PRAYER
FOUNDATIONS

RaJean Thayer Vawter

Vawtermark Publications

ENDORSEMENTS

During this period of the Global Epidemic, Sheila and I had the privilege of meeting RaJean and her husband, Gary, and spending time with them in their home in the countryside. We were impacted by the spiritual concepts and the teaching gift deposited in RaJean, supported by her books and various articles and regularly written letters.

Having visited India, they both had experienced eastern culture and were praying and longing to continue reaching out to that part of the world. Our ministry in India, under the banner, *Spirit-filled Churches of India*, and in neighboring countries, is focused on the global shaping of the Body of Christ. RaJean's approach to the subjects, and her ability to teach in simple words with practical examples, penetrate through the soul and the spirit of everyone who hears them.

Her book, *Prayer Foundations*, is not just another book on prayer. Her step-by-step building up of the prayer-life of individuals and of the collective body is so remarkable that each chapter is a subject in itself. Beginning from the basics and ending with praying for the government of a nation and nations, each subject is meticulously covered.

I have proposed to get this book translated into as many languages as possible to reach more than half of the world population, who do not read English. I pray for the required finance to flow into support of her ministry.

This book is not only a must-read for everyone but also a guide for ministers who teach this subject in the body of Christ all over the world.

Abraham Sekhar
Founder and Overseer
Spirit-filled Churches of India
Global Apostolic Transformation Missions

In this day of global chaos, media deception, public lawlessness, and pandemic fear, the Body of Christ is being called upon to mature to the next level of releasing biblically-based, Holy Spirit-led intercession!

My friend and co-laborer in the Kingdom, RaJean Vawter, has written an excellent book that will serve us well in going to the next level in prayer. She and her husband, Gary, have a long history of effective ministry in the arena of prophetic intercession.

In my opinion, RaJean has given us an encyclopedia on this topic. She covers every conceivable aspect of hearing the Lord and interceding accordingly. For example, she presents the following: intimacy with the Lord; lifestyle intercession; warfare through prayer; apostolic and prophetic anointings in intercession; how to pray for civil governments; guidelines for pre-emptive prayer; strategies for prayer journeys; and much more!

You can easily use this volume as a manual for teaching others and leading them into biblically-based, experientially tested, and Spirit-anointed intercession.

I am convinced that RaJean's book, which is very readable and extraordinarily interesting, will lead you and me into more effective intercessory prayer and will inform and strengthen corporate prayer.

This book is powerful, prophetic, penetrating, and practical.

Jim Hodges
President and Founder
Federation of Ministers and Churches International

The foundation is the most important element in the construction of a new building. It is essential that the foundation be level, secure, strong, firm, and able to hold up that which will be built upon it. I have personally known RaJean Vawter as a friend and co-laborer in the Kingdom for close to thirty years and she is passionate and meticulous in teaching the foundations of who we are in Christ Jesus.

Her book, *Prayer Foundations*, is an excellent resource for those of you that are seeking a deeper prayer walk with the Lord. RaJean brings years of research and more importantly, experience, to the foundations that the Lord Himself desires to build up in each of us. Enjoy the journey.

Dr. Tom Schlueter
Prince of Peace House of Prayer – Pastor
Texas Apostolic Prayer Network – Apostle and Coordinator

ﻬﻬﻬﻬﻬﻬﻬﻬﻬﻬﻬﻬﻬﻬﻬ

True prayer is a personal sacred journey into the heart of God. Intercession is an equally sacred journey into God's heart for others. This journey is never without adventure. In this book, *Prayer Foundations*, RaJean Vawter, as a gifted Teacher in the Body of Christ, shares her Biblical insights into the subject of prayer and intercession.

Also, her personal experiences as a faithful servant of God will inspire you in your pursuit of Him. I highly recommend this book as both a personal and ministry guide that lays sound Biblical and practical guidance regarding prayer and intercession.

Dr. Walter Fletcher
Regional Leader
Dallas, Texas

DEDICATION
AND
ACKNOWLEDGEMENTS

Sometimes things just appear and become usable. But it seems to be a principle of nature that most things begin from a tiny seed. Over time and with the proper nourishment, the seed grows into the form that its Creator first envisioned. That's the way this book has come into being. Reading my first Bible. Hunger. Study. Action. And the cycle has repeated itself over and over throughout my life. With each step, as progress was made, I've always wanted to share with others what God, in His loving kindness, has taught me.

When Pastor Abraham Sekhar graciously opened the door for me to teach in India via live video conferencing, I heard his request as the Lord opening a wide door for service that I was to walk through. And I've developed the habit of always saying yes when God speaks. When the precious brothers and sisters in India asked for my teachings to be put into print, I said yes again.

For this reason, this book is dedicated to all the eager and hungry souls within the Body of Christ wherever they are.

With much gratefulness and a heart full of love, the following people must be acknowledged for their contribution to this project.

- My husband, Gary E. Vawter, has been right beside me as I've grown and learned the concepts and principles in this book. The support he's given has been invaluable. His expertise as an editor is amazing. And his love and desire to do anything he can to make my life easier is sometimes overwhelming. Thank you!

- Pastor Abraham and his team in India have been so patient and kind as this computer-challenged grandmother tepidly took the scary step into 21st century live video conferencing. In addition, they specifically asked me to tell more of my stories which I would not have included without their insistence. Thank you!

- Madelyn Healy joyfully offered to let us use her home and superior internet connectivity for our video calls only moments after we first met. And when the first draft of the book was completed, she offered to proofread it. Thank you!

- Finally, I want to say something about the cover of this book. It was a collaboration between myself, Gary, the designer and his young daughter, both of whom wish to remain anonymous. In keeping with Jesus' words about His Father's house being a house of prayer, He is standing at its entrance, inviting people to come in. He is not appearing as a lamb, because this is a time of war. Therefore, we must learn how to war in the Spirit with the Lion of the Tribe of Judah, Jesus, our Savior, and King, leading the way. Thank you, friend, for your incredible artistry so freely given! Thank you, little girl, for insisting that your daddy put a lion on the front cover.

TABLE OF CONTENTS

FOREWORD

I've had the privilege of knowing RaJean Thayer Vawter for almost 60 years. In fact, I knew her when she was just RaJean Thayer. You guessed it, I'm her husband, Gary.

Who better to write the Foreword to her third book, *Prayer Foundations*? Over the decades I've had the marvelous opportunity to witness the development of much of the content of this book through her demonstration of a life faithfully lived in service to her Lord.

Three fundamental things define RaJean: 1) her deep and intimate relationship with God; 2) her passion for His word and hearing Him speak; 3) her desire to share with others what she's learned.

And true to the book's title, it all rests on the solid foundation of her prayer and intercession. If nothing else, RaJean is a woman of continuous, faithful, fervent prayer. Everything she does flows out of time spent hearing God speak. It's the cornerstone of her relationship with Him.

RaJean was born to teach. And she doesn't require a podium to do so. The whole world is her virtual classroom. I've witnessed her teach while waiting in line at the grocery store. Or there was the time she had a restaurant's entire wait staff and manager at our table eager to hear what she had to say. She doesn't wait for an invitation; she takes advantage of the opportunities others often miss. I know few people who walk out their manifest destiny as consistently and faithfully as RaJean does.

Let me assure you that this book is not merely accumulated knowledge on a variety of subjects. It is knowledge and truth that has been tested by fire and refined in the crucible of life experience. Wisdom can be defined as that which results in the precise and timely application of knowledge and truth. That is a good definition for what RaJean shares in this book.

As readers, we are the blessed beneficiaries of the spiritual truths brought to light by her life-long pursuit of knowing God and making Him known.

I wholeheartedly recommend *Prayer Foundations* to anyone desiring a closer, more intimate relationship with the Lord. It presents you with simple, practical tips and tools to do that by developing a deeper, more committed lifestyle of fervent prayer.

Enjoy the journey!

Gary E. Vawter
Author, *Rose – A Young Girl's Grit and Grace During World War II*
TXAPN East Gate Region Coordinator

PREFACE

This book was never anything I envisioned writing. And only God could have orchestrated its publication.

The journey to the writing of this book began when I decided to follow the Lord at age two, and was given my first Bible when I was eight. That same year, I decided I wanted to teach the Word of God everywhere I could. Since then I have intentionally read and studied God's Word. The more I learned, the more I wanted to teach others what I'd discovered. I expanded my knowledge and understanding through both church and college biblical studies.

When I learned that God still speaks to people today, my knowledge and experience grew exponentially. God fed my hunger by enabling me to sit at the feet of the pioneers of the inner healing and worldwide prayer movements. I wasn't satisfied with just learning; I wanted to experience what I learned and get my feet wet with whatever God was doing. This involved time, effort, and travel. As soon as I learned something, I put it into practice before teaching others. Teaching notes accumulated.

In 2021 my husband, Gary, and I just "happened" to meet Pastor Abraham Sekhar and gave him the two books I'd already written.

Thrilled to find two people who had ministered multiple times in his native India, he later searched for information about us on the web. He discovered some of the monthly teachings I'd written on a friend's website and liked them. He called and asked if he and his wife could come and visit us.

During their visit, he queried me regarding my theology. Satisfied with my answers, he told me that he had a network of more than 12,000 independent churches in India. He wanted me to teach them from my book, *Focus! Fight! Finish!* via video conferencing. Before finishing the book, he asked me what I'd be willing to teach next. So I put together a series of lessons on prayer.

The classes were so well received that the pastors in India wanted the lessons published as a book, even though videos of each class had been archived on the Network's YouTube channel. And that is how the book you are holding in your hands came into being. It exists because of Pastor Abraham and the hungry, teachable believers in India.

The eight-year-old child in me is rejoicing!

1

INTRODUCTION

When Jesus Christ of Nazareth was born, one of the world religions was Judaism. It was a religion that was:

- Fundamental
- Sound
- Scriptural
- Formed
- Organized
- It revealed the nature of God
- It promised redemption through a Messiah.

Sounds pretty good, doesn't it? But there was something strange about it. They had all this revelation of God and an incredible amount of prophecy about the coming Deliverer, yet no one in that religion knew that Christ had come. There is no record that any of those religious people even went to find Him.

However, there is a record that some pagan men knew about his birth and sought to find Him (Matthew 2:1-12). God gave these "pagans" a star in the sky to guide them to a new "King of the Jews." This star did not appear where we might expect it. It appeared to pagan men in a pagan land - far away from the:

- Holy Land
- Holy city
- Holy temple
- Holy religion
- Holy scriptures
- Holy people
- Holy priests
- Everything holy.

Somehow, the shining of that star stirred up these pagan men in such a way that they couldn't get the idea out of their minds that a special King of the Jews was being born. How much God revealed to them or what means He used, we don't know. All we know is that they were willing to leave the safety of their own country and, at their own expense, travel for who knows how long or how far to a strange little place in the Middle East, looking for this King.

These pagan wise men had a living vision, a heavenly star. And the Jewish religionists had the Book of Scriptures. Which do you prefer to have - the Scriptures or the star?

It is best to have both.

Hopefully, you have the Book. You probably know it better than I do. But, somehow, someway, there's a star shining inside you that is begging for attention. You know that as wonderful as the Bible is, it is wonderful ONLY because of Who it talks about. And that is the Person who said, *My sheep hear My voice, and I know them, and they follow Me* (John 10:27). He didn't say, "Maybe they will hear My voice," or "Once in a while they'll hear My voice," or "Only the priest or the preacher will hear My voice." He said they hear Him! Period. Three times in John chapter 10 alone, Jesus said we hear Him! Yet many believers don't really believe this - or, at least, they don't take advantage of it. And many have weird ideas about how God speaks to them, when and where.

Sadly, some also have a dark star inside that has caused them to be discouraged because they pray and pray and pray and don't see very many answers. Or only once in a while, they see the results. Specific answered prayer is not an every day, or even an every week, occurrence. If this is you, keep in mind that you are on a journey. You've seen the star promising a close, personal, intimate relationship with the King of Kings and you want it. But how can you get it? What about all those unanswered prayers?

First, we each must ask the question, "Besides wanting to glorify God, what do I want to do in life?" If you're reading this, I'm guessing that your response is that you want to follow Him, be like Him and do what He did. We know from scripture a little of what He did when He walked the earth in bodily form. But what is He doing now? Hebrews 7:25 tells us that He always lives to make intercession for us and that is how we're saved and how we draw near to Him. So, if He's been praying for nearly 2,000 years and that's what He's doing right now and we're supposed to be able to hear Him, doesn't it make sense to listen to how and what He's praying so we can copy Him? Doesn't it make sense to ask Him, "How do you want me to pray about this situation or burden or person?"

The fact is, we need a word from God on how to pray for every situation and person, and we need to recognize that change can and will happen. We also need to listen for when that prayer or method of praying needs to change. We need to be so conscious of this that, when we don't get a word, we don't move. We wait. In John 10:27 Jesus linked our ability to follow Him with hearing His voice. So, just how does God speak to us

> We need a word from God on how to pray.

today? Most people answer that question by saying, *"In a still small voice"* as found in 1 Kings 19:12. And they are right; God did speak at that time with a still, small voice which probably sounded even quieter because of the tremendous noise of the preceding earthquake and fire! But that was only on one occasion! The rest of the time in scripture, He apparently spoke in a normal-sounding voice - except for when He roared, shouted or used a loud voice depending on the translation in each of these passages: Jeremiah 25:30, Zephaniah 3:17, Matthew 27:46, Mark 15:34, Luke 23:46, and John 11:43.

We always need to be careful to make sure our beliefs and doctrine are based on scripture, context, and the totality of God's revealed word. We're careful to do so when we read about Jesus using His spit to heal a person (John 9:6) which is why today, we don't bottle our saliva to anoint people with or have a Church of the Holy Spit. So why do we do that with the one instance when scripture reveals that God spoke with a "still, small voice?" To date, I have found - in scripture - 15 different ways God speaks to His children which we'll look at in the next chapter.

In the meantime, let's look at the pagan wise men again. They saw the star, knew its interpretation, but assumed that the logical thing to do was to go to Jerusalem, the capital of the nation from which this promised King of the Jews was supposed to come. The place where the holy temple was. They didn't get this direction from the star or by revelation from God. They assumed; they figured it out on their own. They got distracted and misled by their natural minds. Because of this, they nearly caused the death of the baby King and it did cost the lives of many such innocents in Bethlehem (Matthew 2:16-18).

Many times, we have the vision, but then we get caught up in our own natural mind, get distracted and misled by natural concepts and reasoning and we get off the right track. Whenever this happens, we need to do what the wise men did when they got to Jerusalem and realized their error.

In Jerusalem, they were corrected by the scriptures. It was from scripture that they learned where they should have gone; that what they should have done was go to Bethlehem. If they'd just kept following the star instead of letting themselves get caught up in their own logic, they'd have gotten there sooner and with fewer problems. But when they humbled themselves for instruction and acted on the scripture, the star appeared again. In fact, it led them to the exact location! (Matthew 2:9)

LIVING VISION ALWAYS GOES ALONG
WITH THE SCRIPTURES

My sheep hear My voice, and I know them, and they follow Me (John 10:27).

Prayer is two-way communication with God. When Christians spend most of their prayer time talking to God, they miss the best of what God wants to give. God delights in talking with His children! It is up to us to listen!

This book is all about hearing God, following Him, and acting on what He tells us. Through scripture and experience, we can avoid many mistakes. Having studied scripture for more than 70 years, listening to His voice for more than 50 years, and gaining much experience within the larger body of Christ, I offer these chapters so that you don't have to learn everything the hard way. Enjoy!

2

HOW GOD SPEAKS

**God speaks from His dwelling place - the heart
of believers** (Psalm 27:8; Hebrews 10:16).

When our second son was seven years old, he did something he
shouldn't and I punished him. I told him, "Go to your room and talk
to God about what you did. See what He has to say about it." "I don't
know how to hear God talk," he pouted as he stomped out of the
room. So, I followed him. When he got to his room, he climbed onto
his bed; I went over to him and the following conversation ensued.
"God talks to you from where He lives. Where does He live, Brent?"
"In my heart," he replied. Putting my hands on my heart I walked my
fingers up to my head as I said, "And your heart talks to you through
your mind." Then, running my fingers back to my heart, I continued.
"Then your mind talks back to your heart." I continued to run my
fingers up and down, from heart to head, head to heart, back and
forth, repeating how the process works. "Pretty soon, you have a real
conversation going between God talking to your heart, where He lives,
and your heart telling His words to your mind and your mind talking
to your heart." When I was sure he understood the process, I left him
alone and went about my business. After a while, I heard an urgent call.
"Mom!" It was the kind of yell that every mother knows they'd better
start running. Opening the door to his room, I saw him lying on his

bed, trembling and with a grin like a Cheshire cat. "I heard God talk!" he said sounding awe-struck. I ran to his bedside. "What did He say?" I asked quizzically. "He told me never to do that again," Brent replied. I knew he'd heard from the Lord. But then I queried, "While He was talking did you ask him anything or did He say anything else?" "Yes," Brent explained. "I asked Him how He did all those miracles and stuff." Curious, I got very close to him, leaned over and asked, "What did He say?" "He told me He did them in a very special way." Disappointed, I thought to myself, "Oh phooey, God knew that would satisfy a seven-year-old." I was hoping for a more scientific or adult answer. Instead, I asked, "Did He say anything else?" "Yes," Brent admitted. Then he told me something about our family that I'd never thought of, but won't reveal here. The point is, hearing God can be so easy when our heart is open that even a child can hear Him speak.

God speaks through Holy Scriptures.

All scripture is given by inspiration of God, and is profitable for doctrine, for reproof, for correction, for instruction in righteousness (2 Timothy 3:16). When a friend asked me for some very personal spiritual direction, I felt an immediate check that if I gave her an answer, I'd be taking the place of the Holy Spirit. She needed to go to God herself and not just rely on me. So, I told her to ask God because He knew how to get through to her in a way that she'd know it was Him. A week later, she excitedly came to me. "RaJean! God gave me a scripture! Listen to this!" Then she read the scripture. To be honest, the verse she read meant nothing to me; I didn't know how it applied to her situation. But I quickly remembered that God wasn't talking to me; He was talking to her and He knew her particular "language." When He speaks to me, He speaks RaJean-eze. Not Jane-eze or John-eze.

While I'm a student of the Word, when God speaks specifically to me, it's usually through words that I try to write down in a notebook so I can refer back to them. But He gives my husband scriptures. Verses that are so specific that I sometimes have to repent of being jealous. The point is, God made us all different and gave different gifts, talents, and abilities to each of us (1 Corinthians 12:4). But if and when He speaks directly to us, it will never contradict scripture. Long before I learned how to hear God speak as my seven-year-old did, I told Him, "God, I believe the Bible is Your word so I'm going to study it. If I ever discover that You contradict Yourself, I'll walk away. I don't need a God who can do what I can."

God speaks through angels (Luke 1:11-13; Acts 27:23).

To date, I've learned that people are able to see angels in one of three ways.

1. They see angels with their natural eyes just like they see another person or object.
2. They see angels in a vision or dream. That means that when an angel appears to them, nothing behind the angel can be seen. All else is blocked from view and they only see the angel.
3. They see angels by the Spirit. There is a famous painting that depicts this very clearly. In the painting, a very large angel is watching two children cross a bridge over a stream. The angel is obviously shown. Yet you can also see every branch and leaf on the trees behind the angel.

I often see angels by the Spirit. A woman once told me that wherever she had lived, she asked God to let her yard be a place for the angels to rest from their labor. "What a good idea," I thought. So, I prayed for the same thing. Ever since, wherever we have lived, I've often looked out a window and seen angels walking or lounging around outside. They work so hard, it's nice to provide a place of respite for them.

One week our church held meetings every night. By the fifth night, I knew the auditorium was full of angels, but I didn't want to see them. When I found my seat, I immediately knelt down, saying to myself, "No, no! I don't want to see them. I only want to see Jesus." Quick as a flash the Lord spoke: "RaJean! It's honoring to Me for you to watch what I'm doing!" Accepting the rebuke, I opened my eyes and watched what the angels were doing. It was quite revealing as the Lord simultaneously interpreted what they were doing and why. It gave direction for my prayers for months afterward. I share this story to emphasize the balance we need to attain. Many people get so focused on angels that they unknowingly slip into the worship of angels. Especially when people attribute to angels work that is being done by the Holy Spirit's power. Knowing that angels are sent to minister to us (Hebrews 1:14), some even order and direct them around. Yet I've found no scripture that gives us authority to do that, although we will one day judge them (1 Corinthians 6:3). Instead, I simply talk to God and ask the Sovereign of the Universe if He would let an angel do such and such. While we are to appreciate what angels do for us and how God uses them for our good and for our nations, our primary attention needs to be on the Ancient of Days, Father God, His son, Jesus, and the Holy Spirit.

God speaks in visions (Job 33:14-18; Acts 9:10,12).

A vision is often described as a dream that you have when you're awake. A vision in which God speaks to us, is not the same as a suggested vision someone tells you to imagine. It's not unusual for God to give a vision to one or more people in a corporate prayer setting. When this happens, each recipient needs to ask God what He's showing them and why. Even if they don't get an answer regarding its meaning or application for the group, the person needs to ask God if they are to share it or not. Like any of the other ways in which God speaks to us, we need to always ask if we're to share, to whom we share and when we share. After all, He may be talking to you alone.

God speaks in dreams (Job 33:14-18; Matthew 2:12).

Dreams are like visions you have when you are asleep. Granted, some dreams can be the result of medication or what you ate before you went to sleep. I recommend a prayer before going to sleep in which you reject and renounce all fleshly and soulish dreams, visions, thoughts, prayers, and fantasies. Lay them at the feet of Jesus, then give yourself fresh and anew to the Lord for His purposes that night and the next day. When you have a dream, if you don't automatically understand what God is revealing to you through it, ask Him. When understanding doesn't come, wait on the Lord instead of running around telling everybody your dream and asking if they have an interpretation. Share it only if God so directs.

There have been many books and classes given on dream interpretation. I personally stay away from such books and classes. That is because I believe dreams are too highly personal. The books and classes tend to put people, objects, and even colors into categories. For example, when I have a dream in which I see the house I grew up in, I immediately feel comforted and safe. But the memory of that house does not exude such feelings in my sisters! Many interpret the color beige as calm, relaxing, neutral, and dependable. But to me, beige is ugly, boring, sick, and potentially dangerous. I'm a hot pink or fire-engine-red kind of person.

At one time, a popular method of dream interpretation suggested that you are every person in the dream no matter how good or evil the person. I found that not only unbiblical but dangerous! If dreams written about in the Bible had been interpreted using this method, Joseph would have been responsible for killing Jesus when he was given a dream about Herod and the baby (Matthew 1:13). "Oh!" he'd have said. "God is showing me that I really don't want to father this baby and would even like him to die!" And he'd have kept his little family in Bethlehem while beating himself up for feelings he didn't have! Fortunately, modern psychology didn't influence him. He took his dream literally, got up, packed up, and immediately got Mary and Jesus on their way to Egypt (Matthew 1:14).

So how do you get a dream interpretation? Ask God! He's always the best source for truth. If He doesn't respond to my request for an interpretation of what my dream is all about, I simply ask Him to work whatever He was saying into my being. I decide to trust Him and leave it in His hands. This works well for me; I believe it will work well for you too. In fact, I think I receive more understanding of my dreams than many others do. When God tells me to share a dream, I don't have a problem doing so; but I'm also careful to ask Him who to share it with.

God speaks in pictures (Amos 8:1, Acts 7:56).

This is much like a vision except that what you see doesn't move. You simply see something that is meaningful or symbolic or will lead to God explaining the picture. For instance, He showed Amos a basket of fruit. I have a friend who seems to always get pictures. The pictures she sees are so clear, precise, and amazingly appropriate, their interpretation is obvious. But when it is not, she simply asks God and waits for what He reveals.

God speaks in an audible voice (Acts 9:4,7).

I have never heard God speak to me audibly and have known very few people who have. But this does not mean that it's not possible or scriptural because it certainly is. We read about God speaking to people audibly many times in the Old Testament. But that was also when the Holy Spirit came down upon people only for a period of time - which is why David prayed for God to not remove His Holy Spirit from him (Psalm 51:11). After the death, resurrection, and ascension of Jesus, the Holy Spirit came to live in our hearts. Believers no longer have to wait for something to come down, it comes out of us. As a result, we don't have many examples of this in the New Testament.

When our oldest son lived in Colorado, he and his wife knew God wanted them to move back to Texas. He was reluctant to move because he'd just landed a very stable job and they had a nice house. But he heard the audible voice of God tell him to move to Texas. Obediently, they put their house on the market to sell. No one even looked at it. They waited. And waited. Finally, one day he heard God speak audibly again, "Move to Texas!" He immediately quit his job, went home, told his wife what had happened, and said, "This house isn't going to sell until I go to Texas." He packed a bag, kissed her goodbye, and got on the first bus that stopped in front of their house. As the bus pulled away, he looked out the window and saw the first of several potential buyers drive up to look at their house. I tell this story only to make the point that, when God speaks audibly, it is an urgent, "now" message. At least that's how it appears to me after hearing a number of similar stories. And scripture tends to support this observation.

God speaks through physical sensations (Isaiah 16:11; Jeremiah 4:19).

When the Holy Spirit is present or wants to confirm something, some people get "goosebumps" or similar involuntary sensations or reactions. It might be when little bumps suddenly rise up as when you are chilled. Or the hair on the back of your neck suddenly stands up. That rarely happens to me. But I do sometimes get a feeling of fullness in my head that feels like it's too small for the presence of the Holy Spirit. Others, like my husband, don't get a physical sensation themselves, but can observe it when others do. Isaiah felt his heart (or some translations say his belly or bowels) *resound like a harp*. Jeremiah felt a pain in his chest which he attributed to his heart.

God speaks through impressions (Matthew 9:36; 2 Corinthians 1:4).

Jesus felt compassion for the people who were weary, harassed and scattered. His heart went out to them and He immediately wanted to help them. When an ordinary person feels the same way for someone who is hurting, it is the Lord speaking to them through an impression.

We know it's the Lord because the result is a desire to help them. Satan wouldn't move them that way. He'd want them to just kick them on down the road. His job, after all, is to steal, kill, and destroy (John 10:10).

As we were walking into a nursing home to visit a friend, we saw people gathered around a handicapped van unloading a female passenger who was in a wheelchair. Unfortunately, she had not been strapped into the chair so when the front wheels started down the steep ramp, she slid out of the chair. And there she was, halfway down the ramp on her back with her head on the footrest of the chair! I experienced an immediate impression of compassion for her dilemma and embarrassment. While everyone stood around looking at her, I quickly rushed to her side, knelt down and asked, "Ma'am, may I pray for you?" "Oh yes! Please!" she cried. So I did, finishing my prayer right as the people with a special lift arrived. Only later did I realize that God had spoken to me through an impression - a true example of God using me to fulfill 2 Corinthians 1:4.

God speaks through nature (Romans 1:20; Psalm 18:6-17; 1 Kings 19:11-13).

According to Romans 1:20, everyone on earth "hears" God speak by observing Him in nature. When my children were still young, I was taking them somewhere in the car just as the sun was beginning its descent. I pointed out to them how beautiful the sky looked. Eight-year-old Brock, who didn't know that Romans 1:20 talks about God's "invisible attributes" being clearly seen and understood in His creation, said, "Yeah, well, the sky is just a map of God's character." I wasn't even sure he knew the meaning of character. To hear such a statement come out of a child's mouth was astounding. But nature is one way God speaks to us. He speaks especially to some people through mountains and trees or through rivers, streams, or oceans. He speaks the clearest to me in wide-open spaces. When people want to get away from the stress of their lives and they go to a scenic location, it's because their inner being is crying out for God.

God speaks through lots (Proverbs 16:33; Proverbs 18:18).

The above two scriptures in Proverbs tell us that the casting of lots is not only of the Lord but that it will cause contentions to cease when done in the name of the Lord. Knowing this has come in very handy for me. One year I taught a ladies' Bible study. After about nine months, the Lord let me know that we were to transition into a prayer group because it was time to put into practice some of the things we'd been learning. When I presented the idea to the group, I was surprised to find that the ladies were divided even after they'd considered the idea for a couple of weeks. Some were eager to pray together. Others were adamantly against doing something that could become so personal. I was shocked. "Help!" I cried out to the Lord. He reminded me of these two scriptures. So, I opened my Bible and read them to the ladies. Then I prepared three small pieces of paper on which I wrote one of three possibilities: Pray. Bible Study. Something Else. I folded the papers up and with all in agreement, put them into a bowl. I gave the bowl to one of the ladies to shake it up. We prayed together, asking the Lord to guide us. Then I asked the one person who had been the most vocal about not having prayer to draw one out. Wouldn't you know, the piece of paper she withdrew said, "Pray." And contention ceased.

God speaks through "fleeces" (signs) (Judges 6:36-40).

The word, "fleece," used to describe how God can speak to us, is taken from the story of Gideon. Gideon was fearfully hiding from the Amorites when the Angel of the Lord called him a mighty man of valor. As events transpired from that point, Gideon, who had not yet developed into the way the Lord saw him, was still fearful of leading Israel into battle even though he'd amassed a pretty good-sized army. Needing reassurance, he put a sheep's wool fleece on the ground. He asked the Lord to cause it to be wet with dew in the morning and the ground around it be dry. If it happened, he'd take it as a sign that God was really the One telling him to go to war. This sort of thing just doesn't happen in the natural. Nevertheless, in the morning, the ground was dry but Gideon wrung so much dew out of the fleece that it filled a bowl with water. Still fearful, Gideon asked God not to be angry but would He please do just the opposite the following morning? Sure enough, the second morning the fleece was bone dry but the ground was soaking wet with dew all around the fleece.

When we are at a crossroads, sometimes believers ask God for a sign. Sometimes they let the Lord decide what the sign will be, knowing He knows what will speak to them. Other times believers specify something as Gideon did.

When my husband and I graduated from college, we moved to New York state. We enjoyed living there, made friends, held good jobs, and had our first child. But there came a point when we knew we were at a crossroads and needed to make a decision whether to stay or move elsewhere. If we were to move, where did He want us to live? We looked at a map of the world and realized there was only one place we didn't want to move to. Ignoring us and using various methods, God began to point us to that one place we thought we didn't want to live. So, we put out a "fleece," asking God for a particular sign that He really did want us to move where we didn't want to go. Since our heart wasn't in it, we made our requested sign as impossible as we could think of. In less than two weeks, God gave us the sign we thought was impossible. Within a week after moving, He confirmed that we were exactly where He wanted us.

God speaks through prophetic enactment (Hosea 1:2; Acts 21:11).

The book of Hosea is all about Hosea living out a prophetic enactment (Hosea 1:2). In the book of Acts, Agabus performed a prophetic act when he prophesied about Paul going to Jerusalem (Acts 21:11). When we take the Bread and Wine in communion, we are prophetically acting out what Jesus did for us and how we are to receive His sacrifice. There may be times in your personal life when you have an experience through which you later realize God was revealing a truth to you. Intercessors often use prophetic enactment as they pray for someone or something. When my husband and I dribbled oil around the boundary of our property as we prayed for protection over it, there was nothing "magic" about the oil. It was simply a prophetic picture of the healing oil of the Holy Spirit which we, by faith, applied to the portion of land God had given us to steward.

God speaks with His eye (Psalm 32:8).

I will instruct you and teach you in the way you should go; I will guide you with My eye.

Most of us are familiar with how our mothers often "spoke" to us as children without saying a word by using only her eyes. Either her eyes were smiling, even dancing, showing pride or approval, or she would be giving us what I call, "The Mom Look." You know what I'm talking about. It's the look you got when she caught you doing something you shouldn't. Well, God does the same thing. You may not have thought about it but you've all experienced this: when you've walked into a place, look around and it's like a big frown and the words, "Don't go there" hit you in the face as strongly as when your mother gave you "The Look." Other times you've walked into a room where everything seems to be smiling with love and approval. That's how God speaks and directs us with His eye.

God speaks with His footsteps (Psalm 85:13).

This is much like how God speaks with His eye. It's when He's directed us to go somewhere or do something and every step of the way is obviously pre-planned and pre-ordained by Someone. We love it when He speaks to us this way because the path is so easy and clear. He has big footsteps, so there's plenty of room to not only step but to dance a little. To be honest, sometimes there might be a challenge simply because His stride is so much longer than ours. But this keeps us on our toes and requires us to look at the whole process of traveling with Him from a higher vantage point.

Example: When God told us to move out of the city where we'd lived for 37 years, His footsteps were clear. But what direction was He going? It took nine months for us to see where He was headed. When we finally saw His footsteps, I didn't like the direction they were headed. But I've long known that *"obedience is better than sacrifice"* (1 Samuel 15:22a). So, we followed His footsteps until they led us to the place we were to live. His footprints are so large we felt like we were swimming around for a while, but legal deeds were eventually signed and all that remained was settling in.

> *We must have faith in God's ability to speak, not our ability to listen.*

Bottom line . . . when it comes to hearing God speak, we must remember that *we have the mind of Christ* (1 Corinthians 2:16b). Therefore, every thought must be brought *captive to the obedience of Christ* (2 Corinthians 10:5).

Everything we "hear" must be checked against Philippians 4:7-8 which says, *The peace of God, which surpasses all understanding, will guard your hearts and minds through Christ Jesus. Finally, brethren, whatever things are true, whatever things are noble, whatever things are just, whatever things are pure, whatever things are lovely, whatever things are of good report, if there is any virtue and if there is anything praiseworthy - meditate on these things.*

However He chooses to speak, we can be sure that He will be true to His Word (Matthew 7:7, 8).

We must have faith in God's ability to speak, not our ability to listen.

3

HOW TO INTERPRET
WHAT GOD TELLS YOU

As we learn to hear God speak to us, we must be careful about how we interpret what He says. "Well, doesn't He mean what He says?" you might ask. My answer would be, "Yes, of course." But He insists on using His own definitions for His words – and His own timing.

We have to interpret what God tells us in the light of the Word of God, and in light of what He's told us in the past. Remember that the scribes knew the Old Testament prophecies about the Messiah, but they didn't take all of them into consideration before applying them to their current situation, and to the teacher from Nazareth.

Scripture reminds us that *we know in part and we prophesy in part* (1 Corinthians 13:9). In other words, we may not get it perfect every time. Therefore, we need to keep this in mind when sharing with others and be very careful to just give them exactly what we've heard. A woman I knew battled hard to get victory over fear, depression, and confusion. Shortly thereafter, she visited a church, and when an altar call was made for those who wanted prayer, she went forward. However, their prayers resulted in the lady leaving the church in a state of fear, depression, and confusion. How did this happen? Those who prayed for her heard those three words and began praying under the assumption that she still needed to get rid of those feelings. The woman was too inexperienced to realize what was happening, did not speak up, and spent the next week fighting the same battles she'd already gotten victory over. Plus, she was now quite angry that they'd "put those things back on" her. Her victory returned as soon as I explained what happened and she was able to forgive and shake off the residue of their misguided prayers. Then she had to deal with the things in herself that made it possible for her to be angry with them.

Lest we come down too hard on those caring people who were willing to pray for another, let us look at a similar example in scripture. Look at the story of Paul and Agabus in Acts 21. This story has been used to teach several things that just aren't so - including how God will always bring a man into the scene because God won't allow women to exercise the spiritual gifts He gives them. But that's another lesson. Instead, I want to show you how this story is a prime example of what not to do with what God tells us. When God speaks, we must be very careful about putting our own interpretation on things that, in reality, we only heard *in part*.

Agabus came down from Judea. When he had come to us, he took Paul's belt, bound his own hands and feet, and said, "Thus says the Holy Spirit, "So shall the Jews at Jerusalem bind the man who owns this belt, and deliver him into the hands of the Gentiles" (Acts 21:10-11).

Was this accurate? Did Agabus hear God correctly or is part of this prophecy his interpretation? Well, let's look at the fulfillment.

- Paul did go to Jerusalem and was bound. But...
- Agabus said the Jews at Jerusalem would bind Paul. But, according to vs. 33, it was the Gentile commander who ordered him bound by other Gentiles.
- Agabus said the Jews would deliver him into the hands of the Gentiles. But, according to verses 31-33, the Jews *were seeking to kill him* and it was the Gentiles who rescued him out of their

hand. And they rescued him not once but twice as we see in this chapter and another time in chapter 23.

What probably happened was that God showed Agabus either through words, an impression, or a vision, Paul being bound in Jerusalem and being delivered over to others. And that's it. But he added his own interpretation and it went along with his private prejudices that said, "surely the Gentiles will be the bad guys."

He also failed to submit his prophecy to the other prophets. There were four other prophets in the room. Since they were women, did he fail to do so because of his cultural prejudices? Perhaps this is one of the reasons Paul later wrote when explaining how the gift of prophecy should operate, that *the spirits of the prophets are subject to the prophets* (1 Corinthians 14:32).

What was the result of this inaccurately given word from the Lord? Well, the first thing it did was strike fear into the hearts of the people present. Where fear is, God isn't (1 John 4:18). And they pleaded and wept and cried for him not to go to Jerusalem to the point that Paul felt like his heart was breaking. Fortunately, Paul had his own word from God and he went anyway.

If Agabus's prophecy had been submitted and given correctly, would there have been a different outcome? We'll never know. But it would have made a difference to the woman that I told you about, if those people who prayed for her, had given only what they heard without their own interpretation.

Using her as an example, here's how you can handle an incomplete prophecy. They could have simply told her, "I'm hearing the words fear, depression, and confusion. Does that witness to you?" She would then have had the opportunity to explain how she'd just received the victory over those demonic emotions. Having this confirmation, they could then have prayed prayers of healing, strengthening, and thanksgiving into her.

So, when you hear from God, don't assume you know what He means. Write it down. Mark the date. Ask Him to give you the interpretation even if it appears obvious. One of our sons was out of work for quite a long time. He prayed diligently about his unemployment. One day he heard the Lord tell him that he'd have a job within the week. But no job materialized. He was very puzzled and discouraged. More than a year later, he was telling me about his struggle and how doubt had plagued him. He also told me that the same week his pastor had asked him to teach a Sunday school class. This excited him because, being out of work, he had time to prepare lesson plans. "So, you see," I said, "God did give you a job that week, just like He said He would. It just wasn't a job that paid materially." His eyes got wide, his mouth dropped open and he said, "I never thought of that." And at that instant, all his doubt about hearing God went out the window and he was filled with faith and praise for the God who keeps His word.

Ask God if you are to share what He tells you, or if it is something just between you and Him. Keep in mind that if He doesn't permit you to share what He tells you, it doesn't mean you can brag to others about God telling you one of His secrets but you can't share it. Doing that would be pride talking.

If you are to share it, ask Him when, to whom, and how are you to share it. The first time I taught this lesson, a friend said, "RaJean, this is totally new to me. If God told me to go to New York, I'd be on a plane before it would even occur to me to ask Him, "When am I supposed to go or how am I supposed to get there?"

Always remember to ask four things:

1. If?
2. When?
3. Whom?
4. How?

4

HEARING GOD
AND FOLLOWING THROUGH

What are the most important requirements for hearing God speak? In my experience, there are three things:

1. Honesty with yourself about how badly you want to hear Him.
2. The amount of time you're willing to spend.
3. Your willingness to look foolish and be misunderstood.

HONESTY

Do you really want God's input about every area of your life? Years ago, we vacationed in Yellowstone National Park. Unquestionably, one of the prettiest national parks in the United States. The day before we needed to leave, we were driving through the park when my husband, Gary, bemoaned the fact that we'd not seen any bears. "I really wanted to see some bears up close," he said. Seeing wild bears in the park is not

Do you really want God's input about every area of your life?

an uncommon occurrence. "Did you ask God to arrange it so you'd see some bear?" I asked. "No," he answered honestly, "that would be too easy." Convicted, he uttered a little prayer, as he continued driving along the park road. We rounded a wide curve and there on the side of the road was a mama bear and her little cubs. Of course, we stopped and Gary got all the pictures he wanted.

You might laugh but he was being honest. Are you being honest with yourself when it comes to wanting an intimate relationship with the Creator of the universe?

Are you willing to deal with sin that might be blocking your relationship with the Lord? The sin could be something you really want to do or have, and you're afraid God will say no. God is not a bully of a father sitting in heaven waiting for an excuse to punish us. His answer might be, "no," but it's often because He has something better in mind.

The sin could be something He's told us to do that we haven't done. When God gave us a specific assignment to carry out in 2001, try as we might, neither one of us could make progress on the necessary arrangements to get where we needed to go. Finally, I flopped down in a chair and cried out to the Lord. "What is the problem?" Immediately, He reminded me that earlier He'd told me to put together a folder of teaching notes. I had not followed through, reasoning that I'd do it as soon as we had arrangements made and I knew when we'd leave. Oops! I quickly repented for not doing what He'd told me to do, got up out of my chair, and went to work. Within five seconds (literally) of when I finished, Gary ran into my office all excited because he'd finally been able to connect and make the necessary travel arrangements. Two hours later, I received a phone call that expanded our original assignment and put everything else into place.

The sin could be a burden we're hanging onto because we don't want to let it go. We think we "should" carry it, or we think it's our "lot in life." As an intercessor primarily focused on issues affecting the United

States, the prayer burdens I carry can get pretty heavy sometimes. Additionally, I'm concerned with things in my community, state, and certain other countries where we have ministered. And, of course, there are family and personal issues that are common to everyone. One day, as I was heavily burdened, worn out, and trying to listen to the Lord, He just came right out and said, "Relax RaJean. Take it easy. Let Me run the world for a while." After I had a good laugh at myself and repented of carrying more than He'd given me, I relaxed. Ever since, when I'm feeling heavily burdened, I remember that day and do something to help myself relax.

The sin could be something God has said that we don't want to believe or accept. Now I'm sure you know about Philippians 4:6, *Be anxious for nothing, but in everything by prayer and supplication with thanksgiving let your requests be made known to God.* You probably know 1 Thessalonians 5:18 also, *in everything give thanks; for this is God's will for you in Christ Jesus.* But most people overlook Ephesians 5:20, *Always giving thanks for all things in the name of the Lord Jesus Christ to God, even the Father.*

A friend named Jane, just couldn't accept this. She had a history of fighting with God when bad things happened to people, and she argued and argued with me in a class I was teaching on prayer at church. She insisted that we just couldn't be expected to do this. "How can you thank God for a child dying in an accident who hasn't even had a chance to live?" "How can you thank God for . . ." and she gave example after example. Finally, I just had to say, "Jane, it doesn't matter how we feel about something or what we think. The scripture tells us to thank God for all things. It boils down to, are you going to do what God says to do or not?

We have to remind ourselves that God is sovereign. To be unwilling to acknowledge this truth is nothing but rebellion.

In Zephaniah 3:2, we are given the clearest and most succinct definition of rebellion. It is:

- *Not obeying His voice*
- *Not receiving correction*
- *Not trusting in Him*
- *Not drawing near to Him.*

This leads to the second point given at the first of this chapter:

GIVE IT TIME

We want to spend 15 minutes with the Lord, get our directions or a promise, and then go do something else. Sometimes we need to just sit with the Lord in silence. I was discipling a woman who thought that spending time with the Lord is reading the Bible or journaling her thoughts. One year I was able to get her to join me on the last day of a personal retreat with God. She wanted to talk the entire time. So, I sent her off to the woods to spend time with the Lord by herself. She proceeded to round up her sunglasses, a bottle of water, a foldable chair, a huge Bible, a notebook, pens, Kleenex, and who knows what else she thought she might need. By the time she lugged all that stuff into the woods, found the perfect spot, and got everything set up just right, it was almost time for her to come back so we could pack our things and go home.

Learn to sit with the Lord in silence. When you're in your car, do you have to have music playing or a teaching on some device to listen to? Many times, when I was still able to drive, I'd hear God say, "If you'll turn that off, I'll talk to you." Wow! What a privilege! After my husband retired, because he'd had to work in a busy, noisy environment, he expected noise of some kind at home too. He had to learn how to enjoy the pleasure of God's company instead of music or even continually talking with each other.

Let's get practical. You sit down with the Lord and get still. What do you do next? My answer would be to continue to sit. Silently tell Him how much you love Him. You don't have to pray out loud. God can read your mind. Satan can put thoughts into your mind but he can't read your mind. People think he can because he is very good at figuring out what you're thinking based on your actions. And he has little demons watching you. That's why, when we pray, we must deal aggressively with the demonic in the Name of Jesus. I tell them to go to the feet of Jesus, and then I invite the Holy Spirit to fill me and sit with me. Sing a praise song either in your head or out loud. Focus on Him. If you have trouble focusing or getting rid of everything on your mind, here are three things that might help you:

1. Get quiet. If you haven't already, think of everything on your to-do list and write them down. That way, you won't be worried that you'll forget something and you can temporarily dismiss them from your mind.
2. Read some scripture and focus on what you read. Think about it, whether it's a story or a psalm or instruction from Paul. But don't let the reading of scripture take all your time. God wants you to think on Him. Make another time in your day to read and study scripture.
3. Worship with music but only if you focus on worship rather than let it be background noise. Don't let yourself get distracted by the musical arrangement or the people leading the worship. Pray in tongues. If you don't have a prayer language, ask God for one. It's available to every believer.

There have been times when I've sat with God for an hour and gotten nothing. But at the end of the time, He says one sentence or gives one piece of insight or guidance. And it's worth it. Other times, I don't get a thing. But later in the day, I receive insight or guidance that I needed and I know it came because I was willing to spend time with Him. It's almost as if He's wanting to know if we're willing to just be with Him without getting anything in return. And that's a good question we need to ask ourselves. Are we?

We always want to seek His face, not just His hand.

In 2004, while participating in a conference in India, I couldn't get the women to quit praying out loud when we had instructed them to pray silently and listen for what God might want to say to them. It was the third year in a row that we'd taught the fundamentals of prayer and the need to be silent before the Lord. While the leader of our teaching team was trying to get this instruction across to them, the Lord revealed something amazing to me. He showed me that when we spend all our time talking to the Lord without giving Him a chance to talk back, we open ourselves up to a spirit of poverty. Both physical poverty and spiritual poverty (the worst kind) were so evident in the lives of these women it was heartbreaking. I gathered the rest of the ministry team together and we prayed, breaking the power of the spirit of poverty over those women. Within minutes, they were able to get quiet and listen to God. A word came forth from one of the women that led to a spirit of repentance, and all experienced real breakthrough. It was immediate and very dramatic.

Think about it, where do witty inventions and good, creative ideas come from? The scripture tells us that it is the Lord who gives us the ability to get wealth (Deuteronomy 8:18). When we don't give Him time to talk, we miss what He's wanting to show us. I used to wonder how someone discovered which wild berries were good and nutritious and which were poisonous. Then I read Isaiah 28:26-29 which tells us that it is God who reveals such things. And, because man has too often ignored such revelation, we have settled for trial and error as our unforgiving teacher.

We once met with a Christian businessman who regularly spent time in the Lord's presence. He had a friend who had discovered a huge problem with her business finances amounting to almost a million dollars. This woman had a team of lawyers working on the problem but they weren't having any success, and she was going to have to pay the government a large sum of money in taxes and fines. The businessman prayed and listened. God gave him a word of knowledge. "The problem is in her checkbook," God said. So, he told the woman. Her lawyers laughed and discounted him. An error in the checkbook? That's too simple. It took some coaxing, but he was finally able to convince the woman to let him take a look at her checkbook. He was in investment banking and he knew his way around financial matters and how to scrutinize the checking account of a business. Sure enough, he found the error. The woman fired all of her lawyers, hired some our friend recommended, and saved herself a lot of money. All because one businessman was willing to spend enough time with the Lord to be able to recognize His voice and act on what he heard.

The connection between a spirit of poverty and spending time with God makes sense when you think about it. A person who doesn't bother to listen to the Creator of the Universe is going to be spiritually bankrupt. Their spiritual life is going to be dry and lifeless. It's like being offered a million dollars and refusing to take it because it requires us to go out of our way to pick it up. God gave us His phone number but we often won't even bother to pick up the

> *A person who doesn't listen is going to be spiritually bankrupt.*

phone. Here it is, *Call to Me, and I will answer you, and I will tell you great and mighty things, which you do not know* (Jeremiah 33:3).

BE WILLING TO LOOK FOOLISH AND BE MISUNDERSTOOD

Are you a fanatic for Jesus? An often-accurate definition of a Christian fanatic is someone who loves Jesus more than you do. I'm not talking about taking verses of scripture and getting ridiculous like tempting God by playing with snakes. But Christianity is basically a fanatical, unrealistic religion (in man's eyes). Consider these commands: *Love your enemy. Seek first the Kingdom of God* (before we even think about a career). *Bless those who curse you.* Now that's fanatical stuff.

My mother and in-laws used to give me a hard time because I didn't worry about my children. I worked very hard as a mother and gave the job everything I had. But I didn't worry. They didn't understand that. When our second son was at death's door when he was 11 years old, I didn't worry. I stayed up all night, on my face before God until I received a word from Him. Then I rested in that word. During the critical part of his illness, I was sleeping at the hospital in his room. My mother drove 600 miles to join me. I told her to come straight to the hospital without stopping at our house. When she arrived, she was shocked when I told her to bring her suitcase in because I was going to let her stay with Brent at night while I went home. Of course, she was pleased and blessed to be trusted, but she didn't understand why I wasn't going to hover over him with worry. She couldn't grasp the fact that I wasn't worried because I'd received a word from God that he would be okay; and that I trusted God enough to obey, leave the hospital, and let her be with him.

After learning that God still speaks to people today, a Catholic nun told me that God had impressed on her that there are people in this world who never have a single prayer prayed for them during their entire lifetime. That broke my heart. I told God that if He'd give me their names, I'd pray for them. Shortly thereafter, I began "hearing" names of people I didn't know and I'd ask God how to pray, and then follow through with prayer. But as time went on, the names became more and more strange-sounding to my American/English ears. Just as I was about to decide that I was making the whole thing up, I received three American names. Then I heard, "That you will know that it is I Who is giving you these names, find these women and give them the scriptures I give you for them." What a daunting and scary task! But

I was determined to follow through because I wanted to continue to hear God speak. Looking through phone directories, I found two of them. Gathering courage, I arranged for a babysitter and went to the home of the first woman. When she answered the door I said, "Hello. I'm RaJean Vawter and I'm a Christian. I was praying the other day and God gave me your name and a scripture for you. May I share it with you?" She opened the door wide. We sat down on her couch and I read the scripture. Before I could ask if it spoke to anything in her life, I realized she was crying. As it turned out, she'd been raised in a Christian denomination, but had married a man who belonged to a religious sect. Taking classes in order to join this sect, she realized she was being taught some unbiblical things that she was supposed to accept. But she wasn't familiar with God's word enough to object. The verse God had given me for her was exactly what she needed. Wow! What if I'd not been willing to look foolish?

Another time I was standing in line at a store with a friend. We were talking about how important touch can be in comforting or reassuring people, or just letting them know they are noticed. I made the comment, "Sometimes we just need Jesus with skin on." Two women were in line together ahead of us. When I made that statement, one of them turned around and said, "That's what I need." I looked at her and the Spirit of the Lord instantly showed me that she was crying out for comfort. She had a need at that very moment, and I was to meet it. I opened my arms wide and said, "Well, I'll do that." She literally fell into my arms and I wrapped them around her for a tight, mama-bear type hug. She melted in that embrace and received the love of the Lord and whatever else He was imparting to her in that moment. The other woman, who was her friend, couldn't believe she was hugging a total stranger. My friend was surprised that I would do such a thing too. But God did something special that day - all because I was willing to look foolish.

To be completely truthful, it doesn't always work that way or that easily. Through the years, God has used me to be a blessing to my family many times. Often, they haven't understood, and, being the youngest of my sisters, I've had to endure being scoffed at and put down. One year, we were all going to be together in Nebraska, the state where we all grew up, but no longer lived. I made an appointment for us to have a professional family photo taken together. Just my two sisters, our parents, and me. Oh, my goodness! They thought that was a silly, unnecessary thing to do. What was wrong with taking a picture on our own cameras? Going to a studio would be costly and time-consuming when we could be visiting and enjoying each other. They were really quite upset with me. But I knew this was from the Lord, so I persisted. By the time we finished having our photos made, they realized their error and apologized and thanked me for my insistence. A few years later, they gave praise to God for those pictures when our mother died unexpectedly and our father died a year later.

Remember the story about the struggle we went through trying to make travel arrangements only because I hadn't done what God had first told me to do? Here's more to that story. While quietly spending alone time with the Lord one day, He gave me a prolonged vision. One-third of that vision included the face of a man wearing a certain type of hat. When I saw him, I also heard the Lord speak. "I'm sending you to London to find 'the man in the hat,'" He said. "This man has cobwebs in his heart and you are to clean them out." "London?" I responded. "Can I go somewhere else in England?" Ignoring me, the vision continued. When it was over, I mentally tucked it aside, content to wait for God to give me more understanding.

Now, you're probably thinking, "What?" But by this time, I was used to God often speaking to me in strange and prophetic language. I knew to wait, ponder, and not jump to conclusions. Shortly thereafter, I came to realize that the three parts of the vision each depicted a place in three different countries to go, including what I was to pray and what I was supposed to do once I got to each location. Without giving the details, we fulfilled the two parts of the vision with separate prayer assignments. The last portion propelled us to England on the first flight out of Dallas' DFW airport after the World Trade Center towers came down on September 11, 2001. By that time God had told me where to find 'the man in the hat,' so we booked a hotel room in that part of London.

That first night, we stayed up seeking the Lord as to what to do next. I received the instruction that we were to pray around the old city walls of London. God had given Gary the scriptures we were to pray, and showed him that we could take advantage of a hop-on, hop-off tour bus that followed the perimeter of the old city. The next day, we obeyed everything the Lord had told us beforehand, as well as in the moment, while looking for 'the man in the hat.' He was nowhere to be seen. It was evening by the time we completed the assignment to pray around the city. We ate supper beside a window in a cafe constantly watching the people walking by but not finding 'the man in the hat.' Finishing our meal, we walked across the street to a small internet cafe to send a report back home to those who were praying for us. Standing in line to do so, I suddenly became so restless I had to get back outside.

As soon as I got outside, 'the man in the hat' walked by. I yelled through the open door to Gary, made a hat-tipping gesture, and took off running down the busy sidewalk trying to catch the man. Gary quickly left the shop and followed me as I ran after the man, yelling, "Sir! Sir!" Just as he stepped off the curb to jay-walk across the street, I caught up to him and touched his shoulder. He turned around suspiciously, wondering what I wanted. I introduced myself, "I'm RaJean Vawter from the United States and I'm a Christian. I was praying one day and God gave me a vision. In the vision, I saw your face and you were wearing that hat." As I pointed to his hat, I continued, "God told me that you have cobwebs in your heart and

I'm to clean them out. Now, I don't know what that means, but it's your heart and God will show you. Sir, may I pray for you?" He slowly nodded, still trying to take everything in. So, with him still standing in the street and me up on the curb, I prayed as best I could, trusting that Holy Spirit was guiding my prayer. When I concluded the prayer, I wanted to just disappear because I didn't have anything else to say. I looked at him and he looked at me. Finally, he said with awe in his voice, "My wife will be very interested in this; she prays all the time." At that point, Gary stepped forward and introduced himself. He'd hung back not wanting the man to think we were trying to accost him. We exchanged pleasantries and parted ways. The whole exchange lasted only a matter of minutes.

Assignment completed. We were then free to carry out two weeks of speaking and teaching opportunities, as well as, prayer assignments the Lord had arranged for us before we left home. So much took place during those two weeks, but it was all instigated by God giving me a strange vision and an even stranger instruction. To carry it out, I had to be willing to look foolish and be misunderstood.

What happens when you believe the Lord is telling you to do something, and it turns out it was just your imagination? This will happen, but you tried. Your desire to be obedient did not go unnoticed by the Lord. It's helpful to remember that you didn't learn to walk the first time you tried. You fell down – over and over again. You might have even hurt yourself. But you learned how to walk by trying, by picking yourself up and starting all over again.

Be willing to get out of your comfort zone. If it helps, figure the worst-case scenario, prepare yourself for that possibility, and trust for the best. Following what you hear God say - or think He said - is like trusting the Lord and locking your car. Locking your car doesn't mean you aren't trusting Him. It just means you're being wise.

Are you feeling intimidated by my stories? I can understand that. I used to be intimidated by almost everybody, including anyone who was taller than me. And I'm very short. Finally, I think God got tired of how easily I was intimidated and He asked me a question. "RaJean, would you like to hear My definition of intimidation?" Of course, I did. He continued. "It's looking at someone

> *God's definition of intimidation? It's looking at someone or something more than you're looking at Him.*

or something *more* than you're looking at Me." Ouch! That simple definition changed my life.

Subsequently, I made up a statistic purportedly based on what people think of you. Even though it is not based on scientific research, I believe it is absolutely true. Here it is. . .

- 95% of people are so concerned with themselves, they are not even thinking about you.
- 2 % of people don't like you, and never will, no matter what you do.
- 3 % of people will always like you, and/or love you, no matter what you do.

So, go ahead and just bask in the Lord and walk in obedience. As you mature spiritually, you'll grow more attuned to God's voice and how He speaks to you. There are so many ways He has to get through to you that you really aren't being fair to yourself if you compare yourself with someone else. Let others challenge you or be an example to you, but don't try to be them. They are already taken. You can't be RaJean. That's my job. You've got a full-time job just being you!

Develop an expectation that God is talking to you and you will hear. He's big enough to get through to you. Especially if you're like me, tell Him to do whatever it takes to get through to you.

Remember, there are three stages in hearing God.

1. Revelation -We hear Him speak
2. Interpretation - We let Him define the words we hear
3. Follow-through - We do whatever He tells us to do.

God talks to the obedient.

God increases faith to the faithful.

5

WHY PRAYERS MAY
NOT BE ANSWERED

This chapter lists 21 reasons I've compiled for why our prayers may not be answered. It is short and to the point. I do not claim that this list is an exhaustive one. These are simply the ones that I've discovered from scripture.

The effectiveness of our communication with God is dependent upon the integrity of our relationship with Him. This listing is intended to help you diagnose and remedy possible reasons why your prayer life may not be as effectual as you want.

Each reason is supported by scripture references which are straightforward and, in my opinion, require no additional explanation. However, you are encouraged to do your own further study on any that interests you.

1. Not fellowshipping with God
God is faithful through whom you were called into fellowship with His Son, Jesus Christ our Lord (1 Corinthians 1:9).

2. **Not praying to the Father in Jesus' name**

   You did not choose Me, but I chose you, and appointed you, that you should go and bear fruit, and that your fruit should remain, that whatever you ask of the Father in My name, He may give to you (John 15:16).

3. **Not asking or asking with wrong motives**

   You lust and do not have; so you commit murder. And you are envious and cannot obtain; so you fight and quarrel. You do not have because you do not ask. You ask and do not receive, because you ask with wrong motives, so that you may spend it on your pleasures (James 4:2,3).

4. **Not asking according to God's will**

   And this is the confidence which we have before Him, that, if we ask anything according to His will, He hears us. And if we know that He hears us in whatever we ask, we know that we have the requests which we have asked from Him (1 John 5:14, 15).

5. **Not having God's word in you**

   If you abide in Me, and My words abide in you, ask whatever you wish, and it shall be done for you (John 15:7).

6. **Doubt and unbelief**

   But if any of you lacks wisdom, let him ask of God, who gives to all men generously and without reproach, and it will be given to him. But let him ask in faith without any doubting, for the one who doubts is like the surf of the sea driven and tossed by the wind. For let not that man expect that he will receive anything from the Lord, being a double-minded man, unstable in all his ways (James 1:5-8).

7. **Losing heart or giving up**

   Now He was telling them a parable to show that at all times they ought to pray and not to lose heart (Luke 18:1).

8. Not being in agreement

Again I say to you, that if two of you agree on earth about anything that they may ask, it shall be done for them by My Father who is in heaven (Matthew 18:19).

9. Unforgiveness

For if you forgive men for their transgressions, your heavenly Father will also forgive you. But if you do not forgive men, then your Father will not forgive your transgressions (Matthew 6:14, 15).

10. Neglect of mercy

Whoever shuts his ears to the cry of the poor will also cry himself and not be heard (Proverbs 21:13).

11. Setting up idols – anything you worship above God

Son of man, these men have set up their idols in their hearts, and put before them that which causes them to stumble into iniquity. Should I let Myself be inquired of at all by them (Ezekiel 14:3)?

12. Not honoring the brethren or examining self before communion

Therefore whoever eats this bread or drinks this cup of the Lord in an unworthy manner will be guilty of the body and blood of the Lord. But let a man examine himself, and so let him eat of the bread and drink of the cup. For he who eats and drinks in an unworthy manner eats and drinks judgment to himself, not discerning the Lord's body. For this reason many are weak and sick among you, and many sleep. For if we would judge ourselves, we would not be judged (1 Corinthians 11:27-31).

13. Husband's heart is not right toward his wife

Husbands, likewise dwell with understanding, giving honor to the wife, as to the weaker vessel, and as being heirs together of the grace of life, that your prayers may not be hindered (1 Peter 3:7).

And this is the second thing you do; you cover the altar of the Lord with tears, with weeping and crying; so He does not regard the offering anymore, nor receive it with goodwill from your hands. Yet you say, "For what reason?" Because the Lord has been witness between you and the wife of your youth, with whom you have dealt treacherously; Yet she is your companion and your wife by covenant.... Therefore take heed to your spirit, and let none deal treacherously with the wife of his youth (Malachi 2:13-16).

14. Disobedience

If you are willing and obedient, you shall eat the good of the land; but if you refuse and rebel, you shall be devoured by the sword; for the mouth of the Lord has spoken (Isaiah 1:19, 20).

15. Unrepented sin

If I regard iniquity in my heart, the Lord will not hear (Psalm 66:18).

16. Despising God's word

One who turns away his ear from hearing the law, even his prayer is an abomination (Proverbs 28:9).

17. Acting presumptuously

So I spoke to you; yet you would not listen, but rebelled against the command of the Lord; and presumptuously went up into the mountain. Then you returned and wept before the Lord, but the Lord would not listen to your voice nor give ear to you (Deuteronomy 1:43, 45).

18. Disdaining God's counsel

Because I have called and you refused, I have stretched out my hand and no one regarded, because you disdained all my counsel, and would have none of my rebuke, I also will laugh at your calamity; I will mock when your terror comes, when your terror comes like a storm, and your destruction comes like a whirlwind, when distress and anguish come upon you. Then they will call on me, but I will not answer; they will seek me diligently, but they will not find me (Proverbs 1:24-28).

19. Prejudice, deceit and hate

He who hates, disguises it with his lips, and lays up deceit within himself; when he speaks kindly, do not believe him, for there are seven abominations in his heart; though his hatred is covered by deceit, his wickedness will be revealed before the assembly (Proverbs 26:24-26).

But he who hates his brother is in darkness and walks in darkness, and does not know where he is going, because the darkness has blinded his eyes (1 John 2:11).

20. Touching God's anointed

Do not touch My anointed ones, and do My prophets no harm (Psalm 105:15).

21. Fear

There is no fear in love; but perfect love casts out fear, because fear involves torment. But he who fears has not been made perfect in love (1 John 4:18).

6

DAILY QUIET TIME

Practice the presence of God. Wake up with Him on your mind. If you need help focusing on Him as soon as you wake up, play your favorite Christian music on your phone, or have a scripture card on your bathroom mirror. However, in my opinion, the best thing to do is to wake up in silence and recognize His presence. I, personally, like to start my day the night before. After all, the biblical day begins at sundown (See Genesis 1). After I say my nighttime prayers, I acknowledge that I am already living in the "next" day so I dedicate the day to God and His purposes. When, for instance, I wake up grumpy, I say to myself, out loud, *This is the day that the Lord has made. I will rejoice and be glad in it!* (Psalm 118:24). It's amazing how beginning the day acknowledging the Lord will affect the rest of the day.

Give Him time. It does not matter if your time alone with God is in the morning, evening, middle of the day or night, God will meet you when you draw near to Him. *Draw near to God and He will draw near to you* (James 4:8).

Ask God to show you when He wants to meet with you. It could be at a different time each day. Just give Him time. The busier your schedule is, the more you need that time with the Lord. Since God is the One who invented time, He is able to help you with the requirements of your day by stretching the time or by making it shorter.

Be honest about what you can handle. Don't try to spend an hour a day if you have never spent time alone with Him before. A teacher on prayer told us that when she decided to have a daily quiet time, she set aside an hour. She sat down and began to pray, looked at her watch

> *Lord, teach me to pray.*

and three minutes had gone by. So, then she began to bless her family members by name. She looked at her watch again and only one minute had passed. Next, she began to bless everyone she knew. When she finished, only seven minutes total had gone by and she knew that she'd overstepped her ability. Finally, as the disciples had done, she said, "Lord, teach me to pray." Begin with whatever amount of time you can handle. As you do, your time will automatically become longer as He draws you to Himself.

Trust Him for guidance. Ask God what to read. He will show you by placing a "tugging" at your heart to read a specific book in the Bible or to follow the scripture readings in a devotional book or prayer book. However, be sure you do not substitute a devotional book for the living word of God. Don't fret about whether you are reading the "right" thing. You asked God to direct you, so He will.

Now this is the confidence that we have in Him, that if we ask anything according to His will, He hears us. And if we know that He hears us, whatever we ask, we know that we have the petitions that we have asked of Him (1 John 5:14,15).

Even if you miss His direction, God's word is God's word. He will meet you because of the desire in your heart, as we saw in James 4:8.

When you spend time with God, here are some suggestions:

1. Ask God to bless your time.

Open my eyes, that I may see wondrous things from Your law (Psalm 119:18).

2. Read from His Word.
    He answered and said, "It is written, Man shall not live by bread alone, but by every word that proceeds from the mouth of God" (Matthew 4:4).

3. Meditate on what you read - that is, think soberly and quietly about God. Who He is, what He has done, what He has written. Ask yourself, "What is God saying to me?" Is it . . .
    a. A promise to claim?
    b. An example or guide for my daily life?
    c. A command to obey?
    d. A revelation of sin in my life?

4. Don't try to go too fast or read too much. One verse that you can hold onto all day is better than three chapters that you've forgotten a few hours later. *Your word I have hidden in my heart, that I might not sin against You* (Psalm 119:11).

5. Talk to God but keep it short.

6. Praise Him according to Psalm 150:2-6 - *Praise Him for His mighty acts; praise Him according to His excellent greatness! Praise Him with the sound of the trumpet; praise Him with the lute and harp! Praise Him with the timbrel and dance; praise Him with stringed instruments and flutes! Praise Him with loud cymbals; praise Him with clashing cymbals! Let everything that has breath praise the Lord. Praise the Lord!*

7. Thank Him.
    Giving thanks always for all things to God the Father in the name of our Lord Jesus Christ (Ephesians 5:20).

8. Confess your sins.

   If we confess our sins, He is faithful and just to forgive us our sins and to cleanse us from all unrighteousness (1 John 1:9).

9. Pray for your family and others.

   Let each of you look out not only for his own interests, but also for the interests of others (Philippians 2:4).

10. Pray for yourself.

    Be anxious for nothing, but in everything by prayer and supplication, with thanksgiving, let your requests be made known to God (Philippians 4:6). *If any of you lacks wisdom, let him ask of God, who gives to all liberally and without reproach, and it will be given to him* (James 1:5). *Behold, God is mighty, but despises no one; He is mighty in strength of understanding* (Job 36:5).

11. Pray for those in authority.

    Therefore, I exhort first of all, that supplications, prayers, intercessions, and giving of thanks be made for all men, for kings and all who are in authority, that we may lead a quiet and peaceable life in all godliness and reverence (1 Timothy 2:1,2).

12. Relax.

    Come to Me, all you who labor and are heavy laden, and I will give you rest. Take My yoke upon you and learn from Me, for I am meek and lowly in heart, and you will find rest for your souls. For My yoke is easy and My burden is light (Matthew 11:28-30).

13. Give God time to talk back. Spend the bulk of your alone time listening to Him talk back to you.

14. Cultivate active listening.

7

HOW TO FOCUS ON THE LORD

With the advent of email, Facebook, texting, and all of the other ways to communicate, people everywhere find their attention pulled in several directions all at once. It's often hard to focus on anything. Spending time with the Lord is voluntary so it's often a challenge to do so. Quieting our minds so we can focus on Him can be an even greater challenge. Hopefully, this chapter will help you to do that. Some of the tips listed here are given in other chapters but that is to be expected because they are important.

1. Relax. God will show you when that time is for you and your schedule. When I had three babies, two in diapers, my quiet time varied. Now that the children are out of the nest and it's just my husband and me, I have options. Usually, it's first thing in the morning, and sometimes during the day as well. More than 30 years ago my husband came to me with the following question: "RaJean, I've watched you. You wake up talking to the Lord. I get up, shower, dress, eat breakfast, and am on my way to work before it even dawns on me to pray. How do you do it?" I didn't say anything. Instead, I got out some bright red lipstick and wrote on the back tile wall in the shower, "Good morning, Jesus!" On another wall, I wrote, "Praise the Lord!"

And on the third wall, I wrote, "Thank You, God!" It wasn't long before his "problem" was solved. Doing what I did might sound extreme but it lines up perfectly with Deuteronomy 11:20. Referring to the word of the Lord, that passage says, *You shall write them on the doorposts of your house and on your gates.*

2. Review the activities of your day with the Lord each night before you go to sleep. Repent as needed.

3. From time to time, schedule a special time to spend with just the Lord – no devotional or Bible reading, no music, no other distractions. The more your mind wanders, the more time you'll need.

4. When you spend time with the Lord, have pen and paper handy so that when your focus is interrupted by something you need to do, you can write it down and go back to focusing on the Lord. Plus, the Lord may give you a word that you will want to write down so that you can refer back to it. I keep a small notebook beside the chair I usually sit in for my quiet time. I call it my book for "'Writin' Down Talk."

5. Lay your needs, problems and prayer lists down and thank the Lord for what He has done. This is praise.

6. Be willing to just sit with the Lord with nothing else going on. But don't let your mind go blank. Follow Philippians 4:8: *Finally, brethren, whatever things are true, whatever things are noble, whatever things are just, whatever things are pure, whatever things are lovely, whatever things are of good report, if there is any virtue and if there is anything praiseworthy – meditate on these things* (emphasis - mine).

7. Forget about yourself and concentrate on His worthiness, His character – as opposed to what He does. This is worship.

8. Surrender totally to the Lord.

9. Surround yourself with silence for as much of the day as possible. Turn off the radio, CD players, television, smartphones, iPods, etc.

10. Memorize scripture. *You shall bind them as a sign on your hand, and they shall be as frontlets between your eyes* (Deuteronomy 6:8, talking about the Word of God).

11. Give yourself visual stimuli that will draw you to the Lord. *You shall write them on the doorposts of your house and on your gates* (Deuteronomy 6:9, talking about the Word of God).

   When our oldest son was still very young, I laid down with him one afternoon to help him take a nap. As I lay there, I realized that the last thing he saw before going to sleep was the space between the closet and the ceiling. I wanted him to go to sleep thinking of Jesus. So I purchased a few, small, inexpensive pictures of Jesus and attached them to that empty space above the closet.

12. Don't hurry your time with the Lord.

13. Don't feel sorry for yourself.

14. Speak to unbelievers about the Lord.

15. Read the Gospels over and over and over and over.

16. Receive everyone as a gift from the Lord.

8

POSITIONS OF PRAYER

Typically, when we envision someone praying, we see them sitting with fingers interlaced, head bowed, and eyes closed. But, as you will see in the following examples of prayer found throughout scripture, that is just one of many physical positions of prayer. Often multiple positions of prayer were used during the course of the individual's prayer or intercession.

SITTING - Pondering, comforting, dialogue. A position of rest. It's saying, "God, I'm at peace with you."

Then King David went in and sat before the Lord; and he said, "Who am I, O Lord God? And what is my house, that You have brought me this far? And yet this was a small thing in Your sight, O God; and You have also spoken of Your servant's house for a great while to come, and have regarded me according to the rank of a man of high degree, O Lord God" (1 Chronicles 17:16-17).

KNEELING - Dependency, surrender, submission, humility, giving birth, petition.

At the evening sacrifice I arose from my fasting; and having torn my garment and my robe, I fell on my knees and spread out my hands to the Lord my God (Ezra 9:5).

WALKING - Warring, watching, battle, a posture of war.

He returned and walked back and forth in the house, and again went up and stretched himself out on him; then the child sneezed seven times, and the child opened his eyes [Bringing to life the child of the Shunammite woman.] (2 Kings 4:35).

STANDING - Respect, victory, often corporate, a stance of readiness. The first time Handel's "Hallelujah Chorus" was sung, the King, who was in the audience, stood. When the king stands, everybody else stands. Since then, it is a tradition to stand during a performance of that piece of music.

Stand up and bless the Lord your God forever and ever! [So said the Levites to the children of Israel after confessing their sins and the reading of the Law.] (Nehemiah 9:5)

BOWING - Honor, reverence, worship, humility, respect.

So Moses made haste and bowed his head toward the earth and worshipped (Exodus 34:8).

At the name of Jesus every knee should bow, of those in heaven, and of those on earth, and of those under the earth (Philippians 2:10).

WITH UPLIFTED HANDS - Worship, surrender, beseeching, praise.

Then Solomon stood before the altar of the Lord in the presence of all the assembly of Israel and spread out his hands (for Solomon had made a bronze platform five cubits long, five cubits wide, and three cubits high, and had set it in the midst of the court; and he stood on it, knelt down on his knees before all the assembly of Israel, and spread out his hands toward heaven) (2 Chronicles 6:12-13).

PROSTRATE – Heart-rending, beseeching, repentance, desperation.

Then Joshua tore his clothes, and fell to the earth on his face before the ark of the Lord until evening, he and the elders of Israel; and they put dust on their heads (Joshua 7:6).

He went a little farther and fell on His face, and prayed, saying, "O My Father, if it is possible, let this cup pass from Me; nevertheless, not as I will, but as You will" (Matthew 26:39).

9

INTERCESSION

Praying always with all prayer and supplication in the Spirit, being watchful to this end with all perseverance and supplication for all the saints (Ephesians 6:18).

Therefore, I exhort first of all that supplications, prayers, intercessions, and giving of thanks be made for all men (1 Timothy 2:1).

Intercession by definition is putting yourself in the place of another, intervening in another person's affairs. A good example is how Jesus intervened, came between God and man in our affairs. Even now, the Holy Spirit also intercedes for us.

Likewise, the Spirit also helps in our weaknesses. For we do not know what we should pray for as we ought, but the Spirit Himself makes intercession for us with groanings which cannot be uttered. Now He who searches the hearts knows what the mind of the Spirit is, because He makes intercession for the saints according to the will of God (Romans 8:26-27).

After receiving salvation, we are to follow in the footsteps of Jesus. We all know that this means to follow His behavior, His actions, His words. But what has He been doing for nearly 2,000 years?

> What has He been doing for nearly 2,000 years?

Therefore, He is also able to save to the uttermost those who come to God through Him, since He always lives to make intercession for them (Hebrews 7:25).

Following in the footsteps of Jesus would, therefore, mean that we learn about and engage in intercession. "Well, we all pray," you might say. But 1 Timothy 2:1, given above, makes clear that there is a difference between supplications, prayers, intercession, and thanksgiving. So how is intercession different than simply praying for ourselves and others, lifting up our requests (supplications) to the Father? I learned the difference years ago when I asked a friend to intercede for me in a struggle I was experiencing. She brought me up short when she said, "I can't promise that. I'll pray for you and ask the Lord to give me intercession for you, but since I haven't asked yet, I can't promise that."

Investigating the difference between prayer and intercession, I learned that intercession is more than praying the scriptures and being a prayer warrior. It is freely given, but not necessarily when we want. It is a willingness to get involved, even to get dirty if required. Many people define intercessors as a special class of Christians and say that what they do in prayer is not for everyone. But, have you ever prayed the Lord's Prayer? If so, then you've prayed, *Your kingdom come, Your will be done, as in Heaven, so also on the earth* (Luke 11:2). That's an invitation to intercede and get involved. You just committed to spending time with the Lord developing an intimate relationship with Him, hearing what Jesus is praying, and letting the Holy Spirit reveal to you what and how to pray. You just volunteered to be an intercessor!

Since my friend surprised me with her response, I scoured the scriptures to see if what she said was true. I found that, as stated above, intercession is always accompanied by personal involvement and identification with the one being prayed for.

Remember the story I told in Chapter 4 (Hearing God and Following Through), about praying and receiving three women's names, finding them, and giving each a scripture? I received their names because I'd told the Lord that I would intercede for people who needed prayer. To truly do that, I had to get involved in their lives. Intercession is not sitting back and pointing the finger at "you" or "they." It is not self-righteous self-justification. It is not forgetting how much we have had to be forgiven.

Seek the Lord, all you meek of the earth, who have upheld His justice. Seek righteousness, seek humility. It may be that you will be hidden in the day of the Lord's anger (Zephaniah 2:3).

I stress this point because, in intercession, you will receive words of knowledge, prophecy, and discernment more often than any other type of prayer. If this supernatural knowledge does not come out of a clean, humble vessel it will be tainted, soulish, and/or judgmental.

A wrong attitude makes a prophecy questionable since God is a God of love and everything He does is done in love. Bits and pieces of a prophecy may be true but the wrong spirit can distort God's message and actually do harm. I think this is why so often in scripture, God complained about the lack of intercessors. I'm sure there were plenty of people praying, crying out to God for help and intervention. But no one was willing to get involved, and they insisted on praying against "those terrible Romans, or Chaldeans or person or political party you most disagree with.

We're the same today. Yet scripture specifically says, *humble yourself in the sight of God* (James 4:10). We're not told to go straighten out and clean up the mess of those ungodly Romans or Chaldeans or whomever. Sometimes we have to ask God what our wicked ways are so we can repent! After all, *the heart is deceitful above all things and desperately wicked; who can know it?* (Jeremiah 17:9). We are just like the people in the Bible, so we lack intercessors.

Lest you get discouraged, you need to know that your life doesn't have to be totally cleaned up to be an intercessor. I'm talking about a heart attitude or mindset here. An intercessor must be in the place where he or she is able to say, "Lord I give my all to You. *Search me, O God, and know my heart; try me, and know my anxieties, and see if there is any wicked way in me and lead me in the way everlasting*" (Psalm 139:23-24). And mean it.

PREREQUISITES FOR INTERCESSORY PRAYER

1. You need to have an absolute conviction of God's righteousness and that God will never bring judgment on the righteous which is due only to the wicked. However, you must also know the absolute justice and inevitability of God's judgment upon the wicked. Study the story of Abraham's intercession for Sodom in Genesis 18:20-33.

2. You need to have a deep concern for God's glory. Study the intercession of Moses when he discovered the golden calf in Exodus 32.

3. You need an intimate relationship with God. As you relate to the God of the universe, you need to be frank, yet reverent. Our goal is to emulate the relationship Moses had with God: *So the Lord spoke to Moses face to face; as a man speaks to his friend* (Exodus 33:11a).

4. You need to be willing to develop personal courage and be prepared for risk. God may choose to use you to answer your prayer, so you need to be willing to get involved (Numbers 16).

5. You need to be aware that intercession is given by God. You cannot "work it up" on your own.

PRINCIPLES TO APPLY FOR EFFECTIVE INTERCESSION

Guidelines from the teachings of Joy Dawson

1. Make sure your heart is clean before God by giving the Holy Spirit time to convict you of any unconfessed sin.
   - *If I regard iniquity in my heart, the Lord will not hear* (Psalm 66:18).
   - *Search me, O God, and know my heart; try me, and know my anxieties; and see if there is any wicked way in me. and lead me in the way everlasting* (Psalm 139:23, 24).

2. Acknowledge that you can't pray without the direction and energy of the Holy Spirit.
   - *Likewise, the Spirit also helps in our weaknesses. For we do not know what we should pray for as we ought, but the Spirit Himself makes intercession for us with groanings which cannot be uttered* (Romans 8:26).

3. Say, "I don't know how to pray." Then die with an act of your will to your own imaginations, burdens, and desires for what you want to pray for. Get rid of all prayer lists.
   - *Trust in the Lord with all your heart, and lean not on your own understanding; in all your ways acknowledge Him, and He shall direct your paths* (Proverbs 3:5, 6).
   - *For My thoughts are not your thoughts; nor are your ways My ways, says the Lord. For as the heavens are higher than the earth, so are My ways higher than your ways, and My thoughts than your thoughts* (Isaiah 55:8).
   - *He who trusts in his own heart is a fool, but whoever walks wisely will be delivered* (Proverbs 28:26).

4. Ask God to utterly control your body, soul, mind, and emotions by His Spirit.

5. Receive by faith that you are under the control of the Holy Spirit and praise Him for the remarkable prayer meeting you are about to have.
   - *He (Moses) looked to the reward* (Hebrews 11:26).
   - *For a great and effective door has opened to me...* (I Corinthians 16:9).
   - *That you may know... what is the exceeding greatness of His power toward us who believe, according to the working of His mighty power* (Ephesians 1:19).

6. Deal aggressively with the enemy - with faith.
   - *Therefore submit to God. Resist the devil and he will flee from you* (James 4:7).
   - *He who is in you is greater than he who is in the world* (I John 4:4b).
   - *And they overcame him by the blood of the Lamb and by the word of their testimony, and they did not love their lives to the death* (Revelation 12:11).

7. Worship God for Who He is. Don't be concerned with time.
   - The ark coming into the newly built temple (2 Chronicles 5).
   - *As they ministered to the Lord and fasted, the Holy Spirit said...* (Acts 13:2).

8. Wait in silent expectancy.
   - *And being assembled together with them, He commanded them not to depart from Jerusalem, but to wait for the Promise of the Father...* (Acts 1:4).
     Then pray believing that what comes to your mind is from God. When in a group, be sure He is through with one subject before you move on to another subject.
   - *Wait on the Lord; be of good courage, and He shall strengthen your heart; wait, I say, on the Lord!* (Psalm 27:14).
   - *But those who wait on the Lord shall renew their strength; they shall mount up with wings like eagles, they shall run and not be weary, they shall walk and not faint* (Isaiah 40:31).

9. Always have your Bible with you in case God wishes to speak to you from it. Paper and pencil are handy also.
   - *Your word is a lamp to my feet and a light to my path* (Psalm 119:105).

10. When God ceases to bring things to your mind, praise Him for the prayer meeting. Give Him all the glory.

DO NOT TELL GOD'S SECRETS

At the time of the transfiguration, we read, *When the voice had ceased, Jesus was found alone. But they kept quiet, and told no one in those days any of the things they had seen* (Luke 9:36).

But Mary kept all these things and pondered them in her heart (Luke 2:19).

Your word I have hidden in my heart, that I might not sin against You (Psalm 119:11).

As we apply these ten points, we are able to come to God and let Him give us who or what to pray for, and how to do so. We must discipline our lives to be intercessors. If we begin to pray this way and God doesn't give the revelation, we need to check to see if we meticulously followed Step 1 and Step 3, as well as the prerequisite information. After all, Jesus was sent into the world *that the thoughts of many hearts may be revealed* (Luke 2:35).

When I learned these ten principles, I literally copied them down and took them into my prayer closet. There, I would read each step one by one and do what it said before I moved on to the next step. When that piece of paper began to wear out, I recopied it and continued to use it until the steps became automatic. My relationship with the Lord grew so much, I couldn't keep it to myself. I invited other women to my house one night a week to join me in this type of intercession. Only two women responded to my invitation, but that's all that was needed. Using our written instructions, we followed the ten steps and experienced God move, guide, and speak. Every time.

One night, one of the women who worked in the office of the local High School, arrived with a heavy burden for a troubled teenager. "Well," I said, "Let's pray and see if God will give us intercession for him." "Do you want to know what his situation is?" she asked. "No," I replied. "Let us pray and you be our confirmation that we are really hearing from the Lord." We sought the Lord on behalf of this young boy, and God gave us specific, precise prayers. The one who'd made the request was amazed at how accurate our prayers were. We all became so excited because we had the confirmation that we were actually praying the prayers of Jesus. Therefore, we knew, according to 1 John 5:14-15, that God would be answering them.

Another night one of the women arrived very concerned because the teenage daughter of a relative had disappeared, and all that the family knew was she had been with a group of other teenagers. We followed the ten principles for intercession. God told us that she had gone to another state, gave us the name of the state, and showed us that she was in a camp for "hippies." He showed us, through a vision, a map of that camp. The person who had the vision described the camp layout and drew it on a piece of paper. By the Spirit, the three of us "walked" the roads of that compound, praying and declaring the presence of the Lord. We prayed that the camp would be used for God's purposes. He gave us other specific things to pray, but I can't remember all of the details. A couple of months later, the girl returned home and confessed that she had, indeed, been in a camp in the state that God had revealed to us. Many years later, I learned that the compound we'd walked through by the Spirit of God had been sold and turned into a Christian camp for young people. Not only was the wayward teen saved, but the property had been redeemed as well.

You may find it hard to believe such stories, or worse still, think, "I could never do that." Please don't limit how far you're willing to grow in the

Lord. Don't put boundaries on how much God can use you, and how much you can hear from God. *Call to Me, and I will answer you, and show you great and mighty things, which you do not know* (Jeremiah 33:3).

Hearing from God requires death to pride. I've found that most of the time, shyness is simply a form of pride or fear because you were told you were "less than" when you were growing up. Neither of these characteristics originates from God. Pride causes one of two reactions that manifest in opposite ways:

- Blustery boldness like Peter.
- Never speaking up. Afraid to make a mistake or say something wrong in public.

Hearing from God requires learning to shut up and learning to speak up. Leaders need to encourage both.

As you grow in intercession, you'll discover what I call "The Five Gotta Be's."

You've. . .

1. Gotta be willing to look foolish and even be humiliated.
2. Gotta be willing to be wrong.
3. Gotta be willing to be lectured to, misunderstood, and misinterpreted (as the Old Testament prophets were).
4. Gotta be willing to pay the price.
5. Gotta be willing to obey.

Have you ever literally cried before the Lord because you want so badly to hear Him speak? If you haven't, could that be a reason you don't hear much from Him? David wrote, *As a deer pants for the water brooks, so pants my soul for You, O God* (Psalm 42:1).

O God, You are my God; early will I seek You; my soul thirsts for You; my flesh longs for You in a dry and thirsty land where there is no water (Psalm 63:1).

Let's look at those five "Gotta Be's" one at a time.

1. <u>Got to be willing to look foolish and even be humiliated</u>. - One year the Lord provided for my husband and me to take a vacation in Puerto Vallarta, Mexico. I took a bundle of Spanish-language gospel tracts which I passed out on the beach. A vendor witnessed the excitement of children running to us to get one of the tracts for themselves. The next day, when he saw us again, he asked what we'd given them. When I gave him a tract, he confessed that he, too, was a Christian and he spent much of his time in the nearby mountains as an evangelist. How wonderful! We gave him the rest of our tracts and accepted his invitation to attend his church the next day (Sunday). Even though we couldn't understand the Spanish-speaking preacher, we thoroughly enjoyed visiting his congregation.

Looking around the large congregation, God directed my attention to a young man slumped down in his seat at the back of the auditorium. Immediately, the Lord gave me a prophetic word for him. After the service, I met a woman who spoke both English and Spanish, and I asked if she'd translate for me so I could meet the young man. We walked to where the young man was sitting and I introduced myself. Much to my surprise, he spoke wonderful English. Gathering courage, I delivered the word God had given me for him that went something like this: "God has a work for you to do and you'd better do it! You have a purpose and a destiny to fulfill, so get up and get busy!" (If you don't think that took courage for me to speak that way to a complete stranger, think again.) He was shocked. So was I.

I learned that, at one time, he was a student at Christ For The Nations Institute (CFNI), a Spirit-filled Bible school in Dallas, Texas. I lived in

Dallas at the time. I never learned the details, but he had gotten mixed up with the wrong people and was involved in something that caused him to not only be dismissed from the school but was also deported from the U.S. Ashamed and defeated, he thought his life was over and that he could never again have favor with God or live an abundant life serving Him. He'd just gotten a new job and his boss, who was sitting beside him, had invited him to church. He was there that day simply because he wanted to please his new boss. We talked for a while as he came to grips with what I'd just spoken to him. Finally, I said, "Do you realize how much God loves you, that He would send a grandmother from Dallas, Texas all the way down here to speak to you?" Awestruck, he replied, "I'm just now realizing that." His boss, my translator, Gary, and I sat with him for a while as he slowly began to realize that his life with the Lord wasn't over and that he still had a hope and a future.

That's quite a story, isn't it? To do my part, I had to be willing to look foolish and take the chance that I'd be embarrassed or humiliated. I had no idea who he was or why God would give me such a strong word for him.

2. Got to be willing to be wrong. If we get out of our fleshly self, we can remember that the scripture forewarns us that *we know in part and we prophesy in part* (1 Corinthians 13:9). Fortunately, when we're wrong, we can follow 1 John 1:9 and repent of *missing the mark*, which is one definition for sin. When we do sin and repent though, be sure to finish that verse. Stay on your knees long enough to receive your cleansing.

If we confess our sins, He is faithful and just to forgive us our sins, and to cleanse us from all unrighteousness (1 John 1:9).

Often, people repent before God, yet can't forgive themselves. Could the reason be that they didn't receive the cleansing this verse promises, and the assurance of forgiveness that goes along with it? You need both forgiveness and cleansing from all unrighteousness.

I spent one afternoon ministering to a woman I'll call Sue. At some point, she confessed a sin she'd committed. When I asked her if she'd repented and asked the Lord to forgive her, she replied, "Yes, many times." Multiple times for the same occurrence of sin isn't necessary. God is *faithful and just*. Knowing that she was sincere in her repentance, I explained how she needed to follow all of 1 John 1:9.

> The work of Jesus is the best beauty treatment in the world.

Then I prayed for God to cleanse her from all unrighteousness. A week later, I saw a friend of hers who asked me what I'd done or said to Sue. Of course, I couldn't tell her because our counseling session was confidential. So, I asked her friend why she'd asked. "Well," she explained. "Sue just looks different and has a peace about her that she didn't have before. We go walking together every morning. The day after she spent time with you, her face was different. I told her so and asked what had made the difference. Sue said she didn't know. Maybe it was because she was using different makeup. I said, 'Sue, you aren't wearing any makeup.'" I told Sue's friend that the Lord had blessed Sue but didn't give details. I knew though, that the difference in Sue's countenance was because she was not only forgiven, she'd finally been cleansed by the Lord and no longer bore the burden of her sin. After all, the work of Jesus is the best beauty treatment in the world.

3. <u>Got to be willing to be lectured to, misunderstood, and misinterpreted.</u> It is really hard when we are misunderstood, misinterpreted, or lectured to. Especially when our heart is to simply hear and obey the Lord. It's even harder when the lecturer is someone who's self-righteous and living the "safe" life. Many such lecturers push us down and then won't let us back up. They are unable to find or say anything positive to us. They are actually convicted by our willingness to "step out of the boat," as Peter did, to follow the Lord. Just remember, at least Peter got out of the boat. The other disciples didn't. Could that be why God in His sovereignty chose Peter to deliver the convicting sermon on the day

of Pentecost? People who try to derail you only think they are safe in the boat. In truth, Peter was the safe one.

4. <u>Got to be willing to pay the price</u>. Spend the hours with God, sometimes not getting anything.

Blessed is the man who listens to me, watching daily at my gates, waiting at the posts of my doors. For whoever finds me, finds life, and obtains favor from the Lord (Proverbs 8:34-35).

In the military when a soldier is assigned guard duty, he or she knows that they have been given a lonely, often-boring job. But they obey their commander and guard their post. So must we.

Discipline yourself to worship either out loud or quietly within your mind. On a church retreat one year, after being shown to our room, my roommate and I were unpacking our things. I also began to arrange the room so that if God awakened one of us to pray in the middle of the night, we could do so without disturbing one another. "Oh," she said, "knowing you often pray in the night, I decided to do that too. But I just can't. It messes with my metabolism." "Yes," I replied. "That's something you have to learn how to deal with." Shocked, she queried, "You mean God doesn't take that away?" No, He doesn't. Or at least, not usually. It's part of the cost you may have to pay to grow closer in your relationship with the Lord.

Others might object, explaining that they work at a job away from home during the day. And that does present a challenge. But, if God is truly calling you to the night-watch, He will show you how to handle it. However, if that is your situation, be prepared to give up something you normally do. While I still had children at home and was working outside the home, I still was called to pray during the night. I didn't give up anything I'd been doing as a full-time homemaker, and it negatively affected my health. That was neither good nor wise.

We need to consider our priorities. The churches I was part of then, taught that our priorities were God (church activities), others, and self last. But I believe that's the wrong order. God first, means time with Him. Not church activities. Therefore, it includes you and your relationship with Him. By making time with God your top priority, you then have more time and energy for your family, your job, your church, your community, etc. I'm always amazed at how much I can get done when I make the Lord the priority in my day. I've learned that the longer my to-do list is, the more time I need to spend with the One who invented time as we humans know it.

5. <u>Got to be willing to obey.</u> If you think paying the price is hard, this one can be really tough also because it often involves other people. Sometimes what God tells us to do is not agreeable to others. In such cases, we must obey God rather than man. If the disagreeing person is an authority over us and they must first give permission, open a door, or do something to enable us to obey God, we must seek the Lord. Prayer can change the authority's mind. Prayer can reveal a workaround. Prayer can enable us to give the situation back to God and trust Him. Through the years, I've seen situations where someone was eagerly willing to do what God instructed but was thwarted by others. When the heart is pure and forgiveness is extended, invariably, God simply provides something better. Take your hands off of the situation, forgive the authority figure, and let God deal with them.

A key truth to remember when it comes to simple, no-frills obedience to the Lord is that *God increases faith to the faithful.*

When I was first learning how to be led by the Spirit, God gave me various kinds of challenges to see if I would obey Him or not. Thinking about what He'd been teaching me while driving home one morning, I decided that, since none of my church friends were going through what I was, it had to be because I was just a "nut." (That was a slang word used back then for someone who was different and a little crazy.)

I laughed and stopped at the grocery store. As I walked into the store, I noticed a man and a woman with two little boys using the public telephone located outside the store. I walked past them, went into the store, and did my shopping. As I was leaving the store, the man and the children went inside. The woman was still using the phone. I walked on by. While I was putting my groceries in the car, the Lord spoke to me. "They are looking for a house," He said. "Give them yours." Being oh so mature, I quickly responded, "I can't do that! Gary would have a say about that!" As I was shutting the car door, God said, "I thought you decided you were a nut?" "Hmmm," I thought. "You're right. And nuts can do anything, can't they?"

I walked back to the lady in the phone booth. This was taking place in the 1970s, so public telephones were in the kind of "booth" depicted in the old Superman movies and comic books. I knocked on the glass door of the booth. Puzzled, she opened it slightly. "Are you looking for a house?" I asked. "Yes," she hesitatingly answered. "You can have mine," I told this complete stranger, using the same words God had used when He spoke to me. She immediately hung up the phone and stepped out of the booth. At the same moment, the man came out of the store with their two little boys. I introduced myself and once again offered them my home. "I live just two blocks away," I explained.

To shorten this story, it turned out that the company my husband worked for had just hired this man who had to move from another city. They'd driven into town the night before. That morning, knowing they had the daunting task of quickly finding a place to live before he started his new job, he'd decided to do something he'd never done before. He gathered the family together in their hotel room and prayed for God to guide them. My invitation provided them with lunch and a babysitter for the boys (me), while they had the freedom to explore houses for sale they'd seen in the paper. They continued to live in the hotel until they could move into the house they eventually bought. On moving day, Gary helped them move their belongings, while I babysat the children once again, and provided meals.

Throughout all of this interaction, Gary and I thoroughly enjoyed smiling and laughing with God, watching this couple learn that God answers prayer. Sometimes in dramatic ways. As this breakthrough happened, our part was just simple obedience to God. When God told me to "give" them our house, I thought He meant to sign over the deed, which of course, Gary would have had to agree to. But God just wanted me to give them the use of our home. I had to simply step up and do what He said even when I didn't fully understand what He meant at the time.

When we take what we know and step out in simple obedience, we can trust God to not only honor our effort but give us further direction and protect us as we venture forth. A biblical example of this is the women talked about in Mark 16. They were just trying to do what they knew to do. They had no idea that God was going to bless them with being the first to learn that Jesus had risen from the tomb. They didn't know that they would be the first "missionaries." They were just following protocol out of love for Jesus. I encourage you to do the same. Learn the Word of God well enough to be able to move around in it. Act on what you learn. If you obey what you know, God will take you further.

You can also rest assured that God will not contradict Himself. Trust Him to turn you into an intercessor. It often makes for a hard, busy life. But it's also fun because you gain a front-row seat in watching what God is doing in His kingdom.

10

LIFESTYLE INTERCESSION

Lifestyle intercession is when praying transitions from what you *do* and becomes who you *are*.

You become so involved in prayer that communicating with God is always there in the back of your mind. When a problem or situation comes up, your immediate response isn't, "Oh! I need to pray about this." You are already, instantaneously praying about it. You could say that talking to God has become a habit, a cultivated response. The discipline of "practicing the Presence of God" is no longer a practice. You're simply aware that God is there. And you view everything that happens to you and everything you're involved in through the filter of the spiritual life – spiritual reality.

Lifestyle intercession is not something that comes automatically. It's something you work at through discipline. It grows by taking advantage of:

- The knowledge that God is ever-present.
- The ability to hear Him speak.
- The opportunity to sit with Him in silence.
- The invitation to take all of your cares to Him

- The ability to pray in tongues.
- The privilege of having a Bible and knowing how to read.
- The need to get direction from God as to how to pray.

For most of us, these are not lifestyle choices that came to us automatically the moment we were born again. We have to work and purposefully make them part of our lives. I want us to look at each of these aspects in more detail.

The knowledge that God is ever-present.

For me, this happened when I gave my life to the Lord when I was 2 years old, alone in my backyard. I can honestly say that I have never experienced a moment when I wasn't aware that God was there. In 2008 I was asked the question, "What is your favorite name or description of God?" I immediately thought "Lord" or "The Carpenter" (because of how much He's had to hammer and saw and chisel on me). But, taking the question very seriously, I meditated on the matter and asked God what He would say my answer was. What I realized, after pondering it for a couple of days, was that my personal, favorite name for God is, *Jehovah Shammah* – "the God Who is there." Most people don't have this kind of experience at the moment they are born-again as I did. Many years ago, the 17th-century monk, Brother Lawrence of the Resurrection, wrote a little pamphlet called, "The Practice of the Presence of God." That pamphlet has helped people retrain their thinking.

When I was a sophomore in college, I discovered the verse, *Pray without ceasing* (1 Thessalonians 5:17). I asked myself, "How in the world do you do that?" Since I'm a visual learner, I decided that in order to obey this verse, I'd need to be reminded – often – to pray. So, I wrote the words, *Pray without ceasing*, in tiny letters and cut them out. Each strip of paper was so tiny that I could cover it with a piece of cellophane tape and still have enough tape on all four sides so that I could stick it anywhere I wanted. And that's what I did. I stuck *Pray without ceasing* all over my dorm room. On the mirror, the chest of drawers, the door of the closet, my headboard. I don't think my roommate ever saw them because they were so tiny. At least she never mentioned it. But, knowing they were there, I would see them, and when I did, I'd pray. This really enhanced my prayer life, which resulted in some major changes. At the time, I did not know that I was fulfilling Deuteronomy 6:9, *You shall write them on the doorposts of your house and on your gates.* I believe this is a verse that needs to be taken literally.

This is a teaching tool that God has ordained. I have used it for my husband, my children, and myself. Do you use it? I often recommend that people go to Sylvia Gunter's website, https://thefathersbusiness. com, and order her pamphlet entitled, "Who I Am In Christ." When you get it, tear the pages out and tape one or more of them on your mirror or a bathroom wall. I've learned that whatever words are in your bathroom, you'll soon have memorized. (Remember, there is a men's wall and a woman's wall.) Put them in your children's room. When teaching at a Christian rehab center for women who had been incarcerated, I got them to tape pages on the inside of each door of their bathroom stalls. And you know what? Without even trying, the women began to memorize these scriptures and it changed their attitude about themselves and God's opinion of them.

The ability to hear Him speak.

I didn't know that God delights to speak to His children until I was 22 or 23 years old. When I learned this, that's when I dug into the scriptures to find out how the infinite God of the universe is able to make His voice so finite that a mere mortal can hear and understand. It is why, whenever I begin a teaching series on prayer, I always start with that topic. I've discovered that most Christians don't know that God is talking to them. And when they do, they don't recognize all the ways He talks that are given in scripture. This ignorance robs them of clear direction and comfort, and prevents them from knowing how to distinguish His voice from the voice of the enemy, or their own voice. I've sometimes been amazed at what people have told me that they "heard" God say – things that are in direct violation of scripture. I've also had people tell me God told them to do something. Once they took a good look at what God supposedly told them, and it is outside their comfort zone, then they tell me that God changed His mind and they don't have to do it anymore. No. That doesn't line up with scripture. One of those times, they simply attributed their own voice for God's voice, or they blame their disobedience on God Who "changed His mind."

The opportunity to sit with Him in silence.

This is often very difficult for Americans because our cultural mindset is predicated on always "doing" something. Many times, I've been awakened at night and know it's the Lord calling me to be with Him. I'll tiptoe out of the bedroom and go to a place where I can have a light on. I get out my Bible, pen and paper, and I'm ready to listen and write. But nothing comes. So, I sit in silence. One, two, sometimes three hours go by before I'm released to go back to bed. When this happens, I'm always curious and wonder, "What was that all about?" Invariably I don't hear anything. But the next day, difficult circumstances fall into place, or I suddenly have insight or direction about a matter. I'm convinced that God simply wants to know if we're willing to just "live and move and have our being" in Him (Acts 17:28).

The invitation to take all of your cares to Him.

I've heard some people say that some things are just too small to bother the Lord with. And I have to ask, "Is anything large to Him?" We need to stop trying to make God in our own image. What about your anger? Back in the 90s, a movie was made in which a preacher became so mad at God, he spent all night ranting and raving in prayer. He paced around the room, yelling at God, saying, "God, I'm mad at You! I'm mad at You!" That scene shook up a lot of religious people and they left the theater saying, "I didn't know you could be mad at God." Well, of course, we can, and often are! People just don't know that it's alright, so they live in denial and never deal with their anger. But in reality, it's like my husband always says, "Who's big enough to handle your anger?" And I always add, "Do you think He doesn't know when you're angry at Him?" I'm not suggesting that angry prayer is how we want to approach God, but only that He can handle it when we do. We can take everything and anything to Him.

The ability to pray in tongues.

I often tell people, if you don't have a prayer language, get one. God wants to give you one. How can I scripturally say this? First Corinthians 14:1 tells us to seek or desire the spiritual gifts. Tongues are one of the spiritual gifts. Ask God for it. He's a good Father and He desires to give His children good gifts. Have you ever prayed the Lord's Prayer? *Thy will be done on earth as it is in heaven?* Well, do you really think your native tongue is the language of heaven?

Why is the gift of tongues so valuable? Because of all the gifts, it's the only one that is directed toward God. All the others are used in service to others. For tongues to be useful to others it has to be accompanied by another gift, the gift of interpretation of tongues. It's an unlearned language that gives you an unhindered pipeline to God. That's why the devil hates it so much, and why he stirs up so much misunderstanding, unbelief, and animosity toward the gift and those who use it. Praying in tongues is prayer that doesn't have to go through your own mind, your cultural training, or your own prejudices and theology. As Paul said, *If I pray in a tongue, my spirit prays, but my understanding is unfruitful. What is the conclusion then? I will pray with the spirit, and I will also pray with the understanding. I will sing with the spirit, and I will also sing with the understanding* (1 Corinthians 14:14-15). I know that we can pray in English (or your native tongue) by the Holy Spirit, but in context, these verses are talking about praying in tongues when it talks about praying in the Spirit. Notice also that it is prayer that comes out of your human spirit – that part of you that was born again.

A man at church couldn't wait to tell me about a change he was making in his spiritual life. Since he had an hour commute to work, in the past, he'd filled that time by listening to teaching tapes or music CDs. Recently he'd felt led to forgo these and spend the entire hour praying in tongues. He said it was hard at first but he very quickly began to notice a change in his life. "Even though I don't get an interpretation," he said, "later on things happen. I'm having thoughts I'd never come up with on my own. Ideas. Direction." He was so excited he could hardly get the words out of his mouth fast enough to tell me about it. Praying in tongues in this manner is often like sitting with God in silence. It's effective.

Let's back up to verse 13 of 1 Corinthians 14 – *Therefore let him who speaks in a tongue pray that he may interpret.* This is, of course, talking about using the gift of tongues in a public setting. But we can use this as a guideline for our private use also. If you're not sure just how to pray about a matter, you can use tongues with full assurance that you are praying correctly. What I've learned is that when you then ask, He will either give you the interpretation or He'll give you His response back. Sometimes you just have a knowing that you were worshipping and praising, or have an understanding of what you were praying about.

One night I felt led to pray for a certain woman. Not knowing what to pray, I sat down and began to pray in tongues. When the burden lifted, I asked God, "What was that all about?" Clear as a bell I heard, "RaJean, you did what I wanted, now get up and go to bed." I giggled all the way to the bedroom because I knew, even though God hadn't said it, that if He'd told me what I had been praying, I'd have been tempted to gossip about it.

Another time I got really mad about something. I mean, really mad. Gary was working the night shift so as soon as I got my babies in bed, I plopped myself down in a rocking chair and I began to rock – hard – back and forth, back and forth. "God," I stormed. "I'm really mad about this. And I know that my attitude stinks, but I am really mad! So, I'm going to sit in this chair and I'm going to stay here until You do something about my attitude. I'm not going to budge until something changes. If this "mad" isn't gone by morning, You'll just have to send someone to take care of my babies because I'm not moving." And I rocked and rocked and rocked, praying in tongues all the while. Pretty soon, the rocking wasn't as vigorous. Sooner than I thought possible, I was calm, and I went to bed in peace. Whatever I was so angry about, God had dealt with so thoroughly that soon thereafter, I couldn't even remember what had made me so mad to begin with. But I haven't forgotten the results of that night. God honors our honesty. I'd admitted that my feelings weren't holy, but I was determined to hear from God. And he marvelously used my gift of tongues to resolve the issue, whatever it was.

For this reason, I repeat, if you don't have the gift of tongues, get rid of all the excuses you've used in the past and ask God for it. It's not a matter of, "Well, if God wants me to have it, He'll give it to me." He's already told you that He wants you to seek the gifts of the Spirit. Some people have told me, "Oh but you know that we all have different gifts." Yes, but as we grow in the Lord, we will each begin to experience all of the spiritual gifts. That's why we're told to seek them. God is saying, "Keep growing, stretching, changing." Why would He want that? Because the fruit of the Spirit is the character of Jesus. The gifts are His abilities. He wants us to do even greater works than He did, so let's start with just doing what He did.

The privilege of having a Bible and knowing how to read.

This is a privilege many don't fully appreciate. It is also a huge blessing. While teaching at a Women's Conference in far northeast India one year, we had sessions where we ministered one-on-one to the women. One woman came to me and asked for prayer that she could remember the scriptures when they were read in her hearing. She didn't have a Bible, and didn't know how to read even if she had one. And if she could read and had a Bible, her Hindu husband wouldn't allow her to keep it. Her situation broke my heart, but made me appreciate even more my ability to read, and my access to the Word of God.

For all of us, the more scripture we have memorized, the greater benefit we have. Memorized scripture is something that man can't take away from us. Being in the Word of God is also a good way of sharpening our minds. Bill Gothard tells the story of how he failed a grade in elementary school. Everyone assumed that he simply had a low IQ. Somewhere along the line, he began to really delve into scripture. The result was a literal experience of the Word being *sharper than any two-edged sword* (Hebrews 4:12). He finished school at the top of his class, went on to college, and he's had an incredible research and teaching ministry for decades.

I was in a serious car accident in 1994 in which I received a bad concussion. Besides now experiencing some dyslexia at times, I began to feel a dullness or slowness in my ability to think clearly. When that happened, I came to realize that I'd slacked off on the amount of time I was in the Word. The antidote is time in the Word of God.

In the United States, most Americans know how to read English. But there are many who don't. Yes, some are immigrants, but it's heartbreaking to see how many native-born citizens can't read the English language. When I worked as a writer for a newspaper, I interviewed a group of adults who were learning to read for the first time. The group was made up of men who'd struggled all through school. As adults, they realized their loss. Most of them had managed to hold jobs, but they said they enrolled in the class because they wanted to be able to read the Bible. It's not unusual for churches to offer reading classes.

I encourage churches all over the world to teach people how to read. Then give them a Bible.

The need to get direction from God as to how to pray.

Getting direction from God on how to pray is absolutely invaluable for anyone who takes ministry seriously. While ministering in India, a little woman came to me for prayer. She was even shorter than I am and I'm 4'10". Tiny lady. But she had a big round stomach as if she were pregnant. I had no idea what she wanted prayer for or how to pray. In situations like this, I often don't want the translator to tell me their prayer request so that what I hear from the Lord can be confirmed by the person I'm praying for. If it doesn't fit, then I know I heard wrong. So, I just got still and waited for the Lord to show me how to pray for her. I immediately had a vision of a little baby girl. I told the pastor who was translating for me what I saw. He said, "She doesn't have a little girl." I prayed some more. I still got a picture of this little girl. I told him again. This time, he asked the woman about it. Unknown to him – and certainly to me – she had given birth to a little girl before she turned from Buddhism to Christianity. She was worried sick that because she was not a believer when the baby suddenly died, that the baby went to hell. She had become so worried about the child that she was experiencing abdominal pain and her stomach had swollen as if she were pregnant. Theologically and intellectually, I didn't have an opinion about this. All I could think of was, "What do I do now?" I felt so inadequate! I closed my eyes again, prayed silently in tongues, and saw the same vision of the little girl. But this time, Jesus was playing with the child. I was able to tell her what I saw, and pray over her. She immediately was slain in the Spirit while the Comforter confirmed to her that her child was safe in the arms of the Lord. The pastor was amazed because he had no idea what had been wrong with her, and I was ecstatic because I had, indeed, heard from the Lord! It's always reassuring to have things confirmed. This story is also an example of how God often uses more than one way to speak to us.

Bottom Line: Lifestyle Intercession is when you move from prayer into hearing God tell you, show you, or impress upon you exactly how to pray for a specific person or situation, using the various tools He's given us for guidance. It is a discipline all believers in Jesus are called to experience.

As intercessory prayer becomes a part of who you are and an integral part of your lifestyle, you may find yourself focusing on one particular aspect. For example, no matter what you or your prayer group are praying about, you find yourself drawn to that one aspect of intercessory prayer.

> *Intercessory prayer becomes a part of who you are.*

One friend was always praying for children. No matter what the topic was, she'd lead out in prayer for children whether it applied to the matter at hand or not. This was often inappropriate as it interrupted the flow of the group's prayer. As the prayer leader, I had to speak to her about this because it showed a lack of discipline. Her focus wasn't wrong; it just didn't always fit in with how the Spirit was moving in the group. All intercessors must learn discipline if they want to be effective in a group setting. But it's not unusual for the Lord to give some people a special burden for prayer no matter what is going on.

Following are some examples of the diversity the Holy Spirit spreads among intercessors.

Crises intercessors. This is my primary intercessory calling. When something big happens either to individuals or my nation, I stop what I'm doing or thinking about and devote as much time in prayer as God requires of me.

List prayers. These intercessors keep a list of people they lift up to the Lord every day. Usually, their prayers are short, depending on how many people are on their list. I, personally, am not a list prayer. However, I keep such a list for my nightly prayers simply because I want the discipline it requires.

Personal intercessors. These are the people you trust enough to tell them anything about your life. When, in the process of praying for you, God tells them something about you, you listen and take heed. I am a personal intercessor for several people. I have also gathered around me people who are willing to be a personal intercessor for me. I send them monthly updates that include the answers to their prayers, as well as, the things I know I'll need prayer for in the coming month. It saddens me to say that very few people do this. I am a firm believer that if you ask someone to pray for you, you owe them a report on how God answered their prayers. To do otherwise is simply selfish. As I write this, I'm remembering a letter I received a few days ago from one of my personal intercessors. She wrote, "It's so exciting to pray for you. One reason that it's so rewarding is that you share the results."

Governmental intercessors. These people do their best to keep track of what their local, state, or national government is doing, so they will know how to target their prayers.

Those praying for people groups. I had a friend who prayed for the people of Kuwait for years. She felt rewarded when she learned that during Desert Storm, our son, who was in the Marines, was sent there. Because she'd prayed for so many years, she had great faith that he would come home safely. He did.

Those who pray for a particular issue. It could be human trafficking, abortion, school curriculum, etc. There are numerous issues that need prayer.

- Family intercessors
- Church intercessors
- Leadership intercessors
- Salvation/evangelism intercessors
- Mercy intercessors
  They often weep a lot as they pray.

- Financial/economic intercessors
- Israel intercessors
- Warfare intercessors
- Proclamation intercessors
- Research intercessors
- On-site intercessors
  They want to physically go to the place they are praying for because of the additional insight they gain when they get there.
- At home intercessors
  They don't go anywhere, but they are faithful to pray at home.
- Worship intercessors

The list of the different "specialties" may, actually, be endless. Often, one type overlaps with another. For example, research intercessors may be led by the Spirit to go and pray on-site at a key location discovered as they researched a matter. The point is not what your specialty is or what kind of an intercessor you are or become. The point is hearing God and following whatever direction He gives you so that prayer becomes your lifestyle.

11

LIFESTYLE SPIRITUAL WARFARE

We are not called to be fighters in God's kingdom; we are called to be warriors. A fighter is someone who goes into a battle or the ring, engages in that fight or battle, then goes home. A warrior is a person who is always on duty. There is no end to the "fight" because he or she is always prepared, always ready, always on guard. A warrior in God's kingdom doesn't put his spiritual armor on every day, because he never takes it off! He just straightens it a little in the morning or after a skirmish.

Practically speaking, how can we remain true warriors when our bodies become tired, and our minds overloaded, resulting in fuzzy thinking and slow processing of information? The answer is found in 2 Chronicles 14.

Verse one sets the stage. Abijah died, making his son the person in authority and with responsibility for the well-being of the people. In the previous chapter, we see that Abijah had modeled for his son how to win at war. He knew and believed God's promises. He was willing to fight for those promises and the honor of God's name. He followed through until the job was complete. He also called on the Lord when surrounded by the enemy.

Most parents hope that their children will go beyond them, do better than they did, and learn from their mistakes. Asa, the son of Abijah, did precisely that, as we shall see by the 21 things he modeled for us.

1. *Asa did what was good and right in the eyes of the Lord* (verse 2). He obviously knew the Word of God and followed its commandments.

2. *He removed the altars of the foreign gods* (verse 3). He did not let it stand and call it "celebrating our differences." He knew what was lawful, even though it came from another culture and was simply a different way of doing things. But he also knew what was false worship to a pagan god. He did not dismiss the foreign god by saying, "Oh but it's only human to worship something you can see." He called a sin a sin, then did something about it.

3. He not only *tore down the altars* on which they sacrificed, but he also *removed the high places* (verse 3). This means he made those places inhospitable for false worship to be offered there. He got rid of the temptation.

4. He *broke down the pillars*, the structure that enabled that worship to take place in the first place so that it couldn't become a tradition (verse 3).

5. He destroyed the temporary and portable means of false worship – *the wooden images* (verse 3). He wasn't interested in transition conveniences. Neither was he interested in the weaning-away process. His solution was to get rid of it! Be done with it! Now! He was building for the future by clearing out and doing the necessary cleansing right the first time.

6. He evangelized. He spoke truth to the people. Once he cleaned out, he filled up the empty space. He told the people *to seek the Lord*, knowing that if they did, they'd have their own power encounter with Him and wouldn't miss those false altars and gods at all (verse 4).

7. He discipled. It's not enough to encounter God; to get "saved." That's just a starting point. They needed to find out what *the law and the commandments* were so they could follow them (verse 4). We don't want just a visitation of the Lord; we want a habitation. That doesn't come without observing His ways, laws, and commandments.

8. He took care of cleaning out his own life, and his immediate surroundings too. He then, and only then, moved out from there. In other words, he took out the beam in his own eye before he took on the sins of those "others" who are "out there" (verse 5).

9. Once the cleaning was accomplished, he didn't sit back on his laurels. He built on the foundations he'd established and fortified those truths and the people God had given him. He protected and provided security for those under his care, and he was not idle with his time or talent (verses 6-7).

10. Though he'd worked very hard and had probably encountered much opposition to his reforms, he gave all the credit to the Lord. In his mind, all he'd done, and all the people had done, was to seek God and He had done the rest (verse 7).

11. He raised up a mighty army with men who were more than just capable. They were *mighty men of valor* (verse 8). When we disciple others, part of our job is to train them, provide teachers and resources so they can become even better warriors than we are. After all, there is no record that Asa was a mighty man of valor himself. He knew that he couldn't do everything alone, but that he needed people of strength around him. As a leader, he did what the Apostle Paul later taught in Ephesians 4:11-13. In this letter to the New Testament Christians, Paul identified the five-fold ministry of apostles, prophets, evangelists, pastors, and teachers. But he didn't stop at identifying these offices. He gave job descriptions so we'd

know how to tell who is a true apostle, prophet, evangelist, pastor, or teacher, and who isn't. He lets us know that they are people who *equip the saints for the work of ministry*. They aren't the kind of leaders who do everything themselves. They edify and build up the believers. And they do this *until we all come to the unity of the faith and of the knowledge of the Son of God, to a perfect man, to the measure of the stature of the fullness of Christ* (Ephesians 4:13).

12. Asa wasn't afraid to put his men or himself to the test, to engage the enemy - even when the odds were not in his favor. He didn't go looking for a fight, but when a fight came to him, he didn't back down either (verse 9).

13. Asa took what he knew to do, how he'd been trained, and stepped out (verse 10).

14. At the same time, he cried out to the Lord with confidence. He affirmed that, even though the odds were a million to 580,000, those figures meant nothing to God (verse 11).

15. He affirmed that he and his men were *resting* in the Lord (verse 11).

16. He was concerned about the reputation of God, not his own. He said, *Do not let man prevail against You!* (verse 11). This is reminiscent of Moses and Abraham.

17. He and his army went against the enemy multitude in the name of the Lord (verse 11). This is a very key point that we need to pay attention to in our prayers and in spiritual warfare today. Before the cross, trusting in and moving out in obedience to the Lord, and doing so in His Name, was essential for victory. Years later, though He never changed, God revealed more openly, the triune aspect of His nature as being Father, Son and Holy Spirit.

For this reason, five times Jesus made a point of giving specific instructions for our prayers and actions. Instructions we need to pay attention to.

1. *Whatever you ask in My name, that I will do, that the Father may be glorified in the Son* (John 14:13).
2. *If you ask anything in My name, I will do it. If you love Me, keep My commandments* (John 14:14-15).
3. *Whatever you ask the Father in My name He may give you* (John 15:16).
4. *And in that day, you will ask Me nothing. Most assuredly, I say to you, whatever you ask the Father in My name, He will give you. Until now you have asked nothing in My name. Ask, and you will receive, that your joy may be full* (John 16:23-24).
5. *And these signs will follow those who believe. In My name they will cast out demons; they will speak with new tongues, they will take up serpents; and if they drink anything deadly, it will by no means hurt them; they will lay hands on the sick and they will recover* (Mark 16:18).

Did you notice the common denominator in these passages? In order to glorify the Father, we must pray in the Name of Jesus. Yes, He and the Father are one. But these instructions are clear. Jesus went on to say that if we love Him, we'll obey these instructions (John 14:15). He explained that in the past, they hadn't prayed in His name. But now, when we address the Father, we're to do so in the name of Jesus. Why the change? I

> We must pray in the Name of Jesus.

don't know and, quite frankly, I don't care. I just want to obey because I love Him. So many Christians obediently pray, *Our Father in heaven,* but then close their prayer with, "In Your name, we pray," in clear opposition to what Jesus said to do.

In spiritual warfare, we must always be willing to let God *train our hands for war* even as David did (Psalm 144:1). One of the cardinal rules to remember is that, while we have a lot of grace with God, *satan is a legalist.* So whatever Jesus tells us to do, we must obey if we want our prayers answered.

18. Asa let God do what only God could do, and he did only what he could do. He didn't try to play god; he did his part which was to trustingly obey precisely as he'd been trained, then step back and let God do His part with the enemy. His job was to pursue them (verses 12-13).

19. Asa took advantage of the victory to gain what God provided by plundering the enemy (verse 13).

20. While the going was good and the anointing for this kind of work was there, he dealt with other trouble spots. He took advantage of what God was doing and how He was working through him. He wasn't just satisfied with a little victory; he went for complete victory (verse 14).

21. After defeating the enemy that had come against them, taking care of surrounding trouble spots, Asa's army then attacked that which had fed the enemy army, that which had given them resources, energy, and power. They took the things of the world and used them for God's purposes (verse 15). *The wealth of the sinner is stored up for the righteous* (Proverbs 13:22).

Unfortunately, Asa did not always follow his own example. Years later, he turned to Syria for help instead of to the Lord. When reprimanded, he did not repent but became angry and sinned grievously against the Lord, His messenger, and the people. When God tried to show him that he was not walking the way he had been, Asa sought help from doctors instead of God. Nevertheless, the model for lifestyle spiritual warfare is provided for us by how he had conducted himself earlier.

THE LESSON FOR US:

- Get rid of everything that is not of God. Every idol, every thought pattern, every supporting structure.
- Look out for others and help them grow and receive whatever they need because there will come a time when you will need an army around you to back you up.
- Grow in faith. Allow it to be put to the test.
- Rest in the Lord.
- Use His name. The name of Jesus is our key to answered prayer.
- Be concerned for the things of God and His reputation. (This requires giving up your own.)
- Don't try to do what only God can do. Just do what God tells you.
- Take advantage of His grace and provision.
- Spread the victory around.
- Then, while you're in the place of victory, be brave enough to go after the things that have fed the enemy within.
- Finally, stay with the program. Don't let pride, anger (hurt), and power undo what you've worked so hard for. Remain teachable, humble, and continue to call upon the Lord and walk in His ways.

ASAPH - AN EXAMPLE OF INTERCESSION IN ACTION
Taken from Psalm 77-84

When I was a child, I was taught that all of our scriptural doctrines and belief systems should come from direct command, example, or necessary inference. This has guided me in my study of scripture all the years since. In addition, I came to believe that even though scholars may or may not have been inspired by the Holy Spirit when they divided up Scripture into chapters and verses, it is still important that a verse 8 comes after verse 7 and before verse 9, and we need to pay attention to that. For example, many people teach that if we resist the devil, he will flee from us. But, of course, that's not true. The scripture says, *Submit to God. Resist the devil and he will flee from you* (James 4:7). The point is that if we aren't submitted to God, we can try to resist the devil all day long, but it won't work. We need the whole verse as well as the context of that verse.

One day I began reading the Psalms that were written by Asaph, who was a leader in David's worship tent. It was one of those times when I just couldn't stop reading after just one or two chapters. The more I read, the more I came to realize that God was showing me something. What was it? I not only continued to read, but I read pretending there were no chapter divisions. The result was a big, "Wow!" Here's what I discovered:

When read in sequence, Psalms 77-84 give an example of a man who was struggling with the dealings of God on his sinful nation. Fortunately, he was persistent in prayer and was willing to work through his own "stuff" until he was at a point where worship musicians could help him further. Fortunately for us, he recorded his progress step by step, so that these psalms give an accurate view of how God often works with and through intercessors.

So, get your Bible out and read the portion given with each of the following points.

THE PROGRESS OF ASAPH'S INTERCESSION

1. Asaph cries out to God in his distress and desperation in Psalm 77:1-9.
2. He decides to build up his faith by remembering what God has done in the past in Psalm 77:10-12.
3. Asaph reviews the dealings of God with his nation in Psalms 77:13-78:72.

4. With his faith now built up, he once again prays concerning the current circumstance. This time, he simply states the facts without the "wringing of hands" or the desperation in Psalm 79:1-7.

5. He pleads for the only thing that can help - God's mercy - in Psalm 79:8-9.

6. He is now more concerned for God's name, God's reputation, and how God has been reproached than he is for the people in Psalm 79:10-12.

7. Asaph prays for help so that the people can give praise to God, not just so they won't suffer, in Psalms 79:13-80:7.

8. God gives him a vision to help him know how to pray in Psalm 80:8-13.

9. Asaph prays in line with his vision in Psalm 80:14-19.

10. He receives victory within his own spirit that his prayers have been heard and that he has touched the heart of God in Psalm 81:1-5.

11. God reveals His heart and His perspective in Psalm 81:6-14.

12. Asaph understands the crux of the problem of the past in Psalm 81:15-16.

13. He understands the crux of the current situation in Psalm 82.

14. With jealousy for the Name of God, Asaph gets angry at the real culprit - the enemy - and prays with authority. He is no longer crying or whining or pleading but is wielding the sword of the Spirit in Psalm 83.

15. The sons of Korah take him into high worship where all he wants is God alone. He is totally focused on the Lord God in Psalm 84.

12

ADVANCED INTERCESSION

And they continued steadfastly in the apostles' doctrine and fellowship, in the breaking of bread, and in prayers (Acts 2:42).

First-century Christians devoted themselves continually to prayer. What kind of praying did they do? Before we look at specific examples, a definition of terms is necessary.

Definitions:

1. The original Greek word for prayer in Acts 2:42 means, *prayer (worship), pray earnestly.* It is from two words one of which means, *supplicate, worship, forward, i.e., toward, denoting motion towards, accession to, or nearness at.* The other means, *to wish: by implication to pray to God, pray, will.*

This is what the disciples did. They were going forward, moving toward God and getting near to Him.

2. *He saw that there was no man, and wondered that there was no intercessor; therefore, His own arm brought salvation for Him; it sustained Him* (Isaiah 59:16). *He was numbered with the transgressors, and He bore the sin of many, and made intercession for the transgressors* (Isaiah 53:12).

The Hebrew word translated intercessor and intercession in these two scriptures means *to impinge, come betwixt, cause to entreat, meet together, pray, reach, run.*

As Jesus intercedes for us, He literally comes between us and the Father. He also meets together with the Father.

3. *Therefore He is also able to save to the uttermost those who come to God through Him, since He always lives to make intercession for them* (Hebrews 7:25).

The Greek word used here means *to intercede in behalf of, from above, beyond, across, for the sake of, instead, regarding, more than, superior to (exceeding abundantly) in behalf of, for the sake of, instead, to entreat in favor for or against, deal with.*

In other words, after His ascension, Jesus prays for us from above, where He is seated at the right hand of the Father. As He prays, He reaches beyond where He is, and across the divide between heaven and where we are. He does so in order to deal with our situation, and on our behalf against the enemy of our soul.

In addition, we learn that the Spirit intercedes for us in the same way. The same word is used to describe the prayers of the Holy Spirit as the way Jesus intercedes for us.

The Spirit Himself makes intercession for us with groanings which cannot be uttered (Romans 8:26).

4. A different Greek word is used for intercession in three other scriptures.

Now He who searches the hearts knows what the mind of the Spirit is, because He makes intercession for the saints according to the will of God (Romans 8:27).

Who is he who condemns? It is Christ who died, and furthermore is also risen, who is even at the right hand of God, who also makes intercession for us (Romans 8: 34).

God has not cast away His people whom He foreknew. Or do you not know what the Scripture says of Elijah, how he pleads with God against Israel, saying... (Romans 11:2).

This is rather fascinating because when you put these three verses together, we find God the Father, Jesus, and man (Elijah) in intercession. That's because the Greek meaning in all three verses is, *confer with; by extension, to entreat in favor for or against, deal with.* And that's just what God did in Romans 8:27, what Jesus does at the right hand of God in Romans 8:34, and what Elijah did in Romans 11:2. They *conferred* together.

Here we have four different meanings for one word translated in English as intercession.

It was the disciples in Acts 2:42, who were *worshipping, going forward, toward* the Lord, *obtaining nearness.*

In Isaiah 59:16, it was God who *came between, reached out*, and *ran.* He wanted a man to do it but couldn't find anyone willing. In Isaiah 53:12, Jesus is the One who *came between* when He was numbered with the transgressors.

Hebrews 7:25 and Romans 8:26 show us intercession by the risen and ascended Lord Jesus, and by the Holy Spirit. It is prayer coming down from above.

Romans 8:27, 34, and 11:2 show how God, Jesus, and Elijah *conferred* together in order to pray.

All of these definitions are what we want to experience, and are often found in progression. We begin times of prayer with *worship* in order to actively *run toward* the Lord and get *near to* Him. An interesting thing happens when we get close to Him, we often automatically find ourselves willing to *come between* someone else and God in prayer. If we don't stop there, God will literally, by the Spirit, let us experience being *seated with Him in the heavenlies* (Ephesians 2:6) so that our prayers come down from heaven to earth upon whomever or whatever we're burdened to pray for. It is from this position, and only this position, that we can *confer together* with the Lord as to how to pray, what to pray, etc.

When in a group setting, this can often look like we've stopped praying and begun to just talk about how we need to pray. But, according to these definitions, it's all a part of the intercession. It is also very necessary so that everyone in the group is on the same page. Everyone knows what we're praying and how we're to go about it.

In a prayer group, especially when the Lord is directing them to perform a prophetic act, it's a good idea for the leader to stop and say, "Now does everyone understand what we're doing and why?" I was a part of such a group of intercessors for ten years. When this group first started, many of the participants were women I'd personally discipled. Because I felt responsible for them, after each meeting I encouraged them to join me for lunch so they could ask any questions about what or how we'd prayed that day. Thus they learned the protocol of the group and grew in their corporate intercession. Eventually, I became what the leader called the "Mama Bear." When new people came into the group, they often gravitated to me with their questions. I always told them, "When you have a question about what we're doing or praying, ask it right then. It's okay and won't interrupt the flow. We want you to fully understand what is going on because we need the prayers that God may give you to pray."

So, what kind of prayer was the prayer of the Bible? Here are 12 specific characteristics given in the Bible.

The Twelve Characteristics of Prayer:

1. It was time-consuming and often included fasting.

As they ministered to the Lord and fasted, the Holy Spirit said, "Now separate to Me Barnabas and Saul for the work to which I have called them." Then, having fasted and prayed and laid hands on them, they sent them away (Acts 13:2-3).

Referring to Barnabas and Saul – *So when they had appointed elders in every church, and prayed with fasting, they commended them to the Lord in whom they had believed* (Acts 14:23).

The church leaders had the congregation appoint people to take care of the physical needs of the body so that *we will give ourselves continually to prayer and to the ministry of the word* (Acts 6:4).

Now she who is really a widow, and left alone, trusts in God and continues in supplications and prayers night and day (I Timothy. 5:5).

This verse is talking about widows who were supported by the church because they did not have family to support them. Anna was one of these women supported by the temple, before the church age.

2. It was earnest prayer.

Therefore, I exhort first of all that supplications, prayers, intercessions, and giving of thanks be made for all men (I Timothy 2:1).

The word here is the same word as found in Romans 8:27 which means to confer with. I don't believe this means just to confer with God. I believe, that we're to confer with one another. Many times, you must first be informed so that during intercession you know what questions to ask the Father.

Gary needed to have some medical tests run. He didn't just go have the tests. First, he did some research on the web to find out more about the procedure so he'd know not only what to expect, but what questions to ask the doctor. If we do this for health reasons, doesn't it make sense to do it before talking to Dr. Jesus? Interestingly, when Jesus was struggling in the Garden of Gethsemane, Luke 22:44 says, *And being in agony, He prayed more earnestly.* The word *prayed* in this passage means to *confer with.* When I was 17, I decided I'd search for good questions. I figured God knew the answers, I just needed to figure out what questions to ask Him. Good questions help us learn. I was always the person in the front of a classroom asking the questions that those in the back of the room were too embarrassed to ask. Interestingly, many of those students would later thank me for asking the questions and *conferring with* the teacher.

3. When the people prayed in a group, they were of one accord.

These all continued with one accord in prayer and supplication, with the women, and Mary the mother of Jesus, and with His brothers (Acts 1:14).

So when they heard that, they raised their voice to God with one accord and said: "Lord, You are God, who made heaven and earth and the sea, and all that is in them" (Acts 4:24).

4. Their prayers were not general or vague.

So Peter was kept in the prison, but prayer for him was being made fervently by the church to God (Acts 12:5 – NASB1995).

The word *fervently* in this verse means *stretched out* and is a picture of a soul stretched out in intense earnestness. The same word is used in Luke 22:44 in describing how Jesus prayed in the Garden of Gethsemane. *And being in agony He was praying very fervently.* The word *agony* means *to strive together, wrestle.* Jesus was not simply kneeling down or leaning against a rock praying, as many religious paintings depict. He was stretched out and wrestling as He conferred with God. The same word is found in Romans 15:30 where Paul pleads, *Now I beg you, brethren, through the Lord Jesus Christ, and through the love of the Spirit, that you strive together with me in prayers to God for me.* This is a real admonition for us to be willing to get so involved in the affairs of another that we're willing to experience agony in prayer for them.

5. Their prayers ministered to the Lord.

As they ministered to the Lord and fasted… (Acts 13:2). This was a real ministering to the Lord, as opposed to asking Him to minister to them. In the process, God spoke concise and specific direction – to separate out Saul and Barnabas, pray for them, and send them out to minister as God directed.

When we experience this kind of worship that is truly focused on Him and ministering to Him, we often don't stay there long enough. Sometimes that's because we have our own agenda and time frame. We think worship can only last 20-30 minutes. Or, "I have an appointment at 3:00 o'clock, can't we stop the music and get on with the praying or the preaching?"

When worship is the first part of a service, it's amazing how many people use this as an excuse to come in late, right before the speaker. After all, isn't that the purpose of such meetings? To be taught something? They miss the point, that the core of any ministry, is to get into the presence of God. In His presence is where you'll learn, grow, receive, and be better able to understand what God has to say to you through the speaker.

Other times we stop ministering to the Lord because, when we get in His presence, we're immediately aware of how unworthy we are and begin asking for forgiveness, naming sins, naming others who need to repent, etc. This takes the focus off Him and onto ourselves. To truly minister to the Lord, we need to go to our prayer meetings

> *When we get in His presence, we're immediately aware of how unworthy we are.*

having already confessed our sins and received forgiveness as well as cleansing. If an unconfessed sin comes to mind during corporate worship, it is inappropriate for it to be confessed before the group at that time. Repentance needs to take place immediately, but only between yourself and God. In fact, it is rude and selfish to draw such attention to yourself while others are focusing on the Lord. It is also rude and selfish to confess personal sin in such a way as to assume others have committed the same sin and didn't get right with God before the service began. Yes, public sin should always be confessed publicly, but not when the people need to be focusing on the Lord. Proper protocol in a group setting is different than when you are alone with the Lord. There is a time for everything.

When in corporate worship, we need to discipline ourselves to keep worshipping, to press in. There is often a point in our worship where we feel that it's time to quit that aspect of prayer and get into the asking part. But this isn't always true. Sometimes what appears to be a stopping place is the Holy Spirit giving us a choice whether to press into Him or have prayer time as usual. The first time I was in a meeting where the leader kept telling us to "press in," when a pause in the worship happened, I wanted him to just get on with his sermon. But I pressed into the Lord every time he urged us to, and, wow(!) did the Lord ever show up! Since then, my experience is that often, it is when we choose to press in that we're taken to another level. Then we get the direction we're seeking or insight into a problem.

A good example of this is found in Genesis 18. When you read the earlier chapters, you see that Abraham had been ministering to the Lord. Then one day, the Lord showed up when he was just sitting in the tent door during the hot part of the day. God gave him the promise, Sarah laughed, and the Lord decided to tell Abraham what He was getting ready to do. He told him His plans for Sodom and Gomorrah, and they had that marvelous discussion, conferring together.

6. Their prayers were burdening.

Paul and Barnabas were *strengthening the souls of the disciples, exhorting them to continue in the faith, and saying, We must through many tribulations enter the kingdom of God* (Acts 14:22).

This word, *tribulations*, means, *afflicted, burdened, anguish, persecution, trouble, tribulations*. It does not indicate the light-hearted, carefree, joy-popping on Jesus, life of prayer with shotgun effects. Instead, it is the serious, not-looking-back, come-what-may decision, serious, obedient, life of prayer both in word and action.

7. Their prayer life was often physically difficult and went into the nighttime hours.

So when they had appointed elders in every church, and prayed with fasting, they commended them to the Lord to whom they had believed (Acts 14:23).

And I, Daniel, fainted and was sick for days; afterward I arose and went about the king's business. I was astonished by the vision, but no one understood it (Daniel. 8:27).

Sometimes our intercessions may bring on unpleasant physical conditions like Daniel experienced (Daniel 8:27). God has told me several times that my body is often a prophetic picture of something. One summer I began to experience a sharp pain in my stomach. I'd pray about it but without relief. I'd fast, and the pain would still be there. I'd eat and it wouldn't go away. Nothing I did worked. Then one day at our Dallas prayer group, we discovered that almost all of us were experiencing some kind of problem with our digestive tract. In prayer, God revealed that, since we were all strategic-level intercessors, He was trying to get our attention about something in the wider Dallas body of Christ. The churches, He said, were not properly digesting their food. Some had too much Word and not enough of the Spirit. Others had too much of the Spirit and not enough of the Word. The church needed a balanced diet and to process the "Bread of Life" correctly. So, we prayed that way. Later that day, I felt my stomach pain again. "What is this Lord?" I cried. He reminded me of what He'd revealed that morning. "When you feel the pain, don't pray for yourself; pray for the church." I did and within a short time, that pain was gone never to return again. Two years later, I had to have some scans of my abdomen. Examining them, the doctor said, "Oh, it looks like you used to have a stomach ulcer, but it's all healed now."

It is important to know that as we push deeper in intercession, the physical ailment will often go away. We don't need to get into a self-imposed martyrdom. It's good to remember Job 33:19 – spoken by Job's fourth friend, who was not chastened by the Lord – *Man is also chastened with pain on his bed, and with strong pain in many of his bones.*

Speaking of bones. . . when I had knee replacement surgery, the recovery process was long and hard. Talking to the Lord about it, He told me that the entire surgery and recovery was indicative of the American church. Therefore, with each new pain or process, I'd ask the Lord how to pray. I was constantly amazed at all the aspects of the church He revealed to me that were in need of prayer. Sometimes, I'd think, okay, I've covered everything about the church but then He'd show me something else. When I prayed, or someone else would pray for me, nothing happened, but when prayer for the church took place, I'd get relief.

It's important to understand that this sort of prophetic intercession doesn't apply to every ache or pain, that we have. When my shoulders hurt, it's usually because I broke a natural law by falling and damaging the bursae. It's immature to try to spiritualize everything. But we can use our various bodily ailments as reminders to pray for whatever is on the Lord's heart at that time.

Like biblical saints before them, some people today have encounters with God that occur while they sleep. When necessary, God will utilize the time when our conscious minds are out of the way so He can speak to our spirit. See the following scriptures:

Yet I heard the sound of the words; and while I heard the sound of his words, I was in a deep sleep on my face, with my face to the ground (Daniel. 10:9).

Now when the sun was going down, a deep sleep fell upon Abram, and behold, horror and great darkness fell upon him (Genesis 15:12).

After this I awoke and looked around, and my sleep was sweet to me (Jeremiah. 31: 26).

Be angry and do not sin. Meditate within your heart on your bed, and be still. Selah (Psalm 4:4).

We used to have a friend who would say his goodbye at night by saying, "Well, I'm going to go seek the Lord in a dream."

I will bless the Lord who has given me counsel; my heart also instructs me in the night seasons (Psalm 16:7).

You have tested my heart; You have visited me in the night… (Psalm 17:3).

8. Their prayers were revealing.

Surely the Lord God does nothing unless He reveals His secret to His servants the prophets (Amos 3:7).

If in your prayers, you do not spend the bulk of your time listening to God speak to you, you only have a one-way conversation. The Disciples' Prayer in Matthew 6 is a very short prayer. Perhaps as an indication of how much time Jesus spent listening to His Father. He told his disciples that He did not say or do anything except what He had first seen His Father do and heard His Father say (John 5:19) and Jesus said and did an awful lot!

My husband and I were invited to join a small group of people in focused prayer. They asked for my opinion on what the focus or target should be. I didn't give them an opinion. I simply told them what the Lord had spoken to me about the matter a year earlier. It was the confirmation they needed for the target God had shown them. This happened only because I'd spent time listening to the Lord, and He'd already revealed His plan to me on this particular matter.

Part of revealing prayers may be in the form of:

<u>Prophetic words</u> – *But God shall shoot at them with an arrow; suddenly they shall be wounded* (Psalm 64:7).

<u>Prophetic acts</u> – Joash, King of Israel, Elisha and the arrow (2 Kings 13:14-19). Verse 25 tells us that Joash defeated the enemy and recaptured the cities of Israel three times, just as he'd struck with the arrow three times. Other examples are The Lord's Supper (Mark 14:22-25) and when Jesus' washed the disciple's feet (John 13:3-15).

<u>Dark Speech</u> (God speaking about Moses) – *I speak with him face to face, even plainly, and not in dark sayings/riddles* (Numbers 12:8).

I will incline my ear to a proverb; I will disclose my dark saying (riddle) on the harp (Psalm 49:4).

I will open my mouth in a parable; I will utter dark sayings of old (obscure sayings or riddles) (Psalm78:2).

To understand a proverb and an enigma (dark sayings), the words of the wise and their riddles (Proverbs 1:6).

And in the latter time of their kingdom when the transgressors have reached their fullness, a king shall arise, having fierce features, who understands sinister schemes (dark sentences) (Daniel 8:23).

Dark speech is often known as something you do that later, looking back, you realize you could view what happened as a parable and learn something from it.

For example, a couple I know went on a bicycle ride together. It promised to be a pleasant time of riding in tandem together. Unfortunately, it did not turn out that way. The wife often found herself bicycling alone because her husband would lag behind, then literally stop and look around. She'd stop and wait for him to catch up, but her husband never shared why he had changed their original plan, or that he wanted her to stop with him. He was simply doing his own thing. When she'd ask, he would say nothing. He refused to communicate or pay any attention to her. After this happened multiple times, she finally gave up and slowly bicycled home, praying all the while. When she arrived home, the Lord showed her that the two of them had just prophetically enacted the story of their spiritual life together. Though both were dedicated to the Lord, she was the one who consistently and eagerly studied scripture, attended Bible classes and conferences, and spent hours in prayer. As she grew in biblical understanding and practical application of the Word, she would excitedly share with her husband everything she'd learned. He would slowly take what she shared, discard what was hard, grow a little spiritually, then stop and wait for her to teach him some more. He'd made no effort to take the lead or study things out for himself. His spiritual life and how he conducted himself on the bike ride were identical. This is an example of Dark Speech.

When her husband returned home, she shared with him what God had shown her. He agreed that it was all true and that it was easier for him to "piggyback" on her spirituality and eager desire to grow in the Lord. He indicated that he expected to continue to live that way. "No," the wife said. "God has shown us this truth, and how we're living isn't biblical. You are responsible for your walk with the Lord, and I'm responsible for my walk. So, I just want you to know that I will not be waiting on you anymore. I'm going to go on with the Lord." She was true to her word, and, for the most part, stopped sharing with her husband the new insights and understanding she gleaned from her time spent seeking and learning. She stopped enabling him to remain a bottle-fed baby in the Lord. When the spiritual atmosphere between this couple became too consistently quiet, the husband began to put forth his own effort to seek the face of the Lord. Yes, he continued to grow slowly, but as the years passed, his speed increased until this couple finally got on the same "page." They now have the kind of spiritual connection with each other, and with the Lord that is a model for many others.

A biblical example of "dark speech" is found in Galatians 4:21-27, where you can read the explanation of Sarah and Hagar, who lived out a profound prophetic dark speech parable.

9. The leaders were devoted men of prayer.

But we will give ourselves continually to prayer and to the ministry of the word (Acts 6:4). They appointed others to do the physical ministry of the Word, while they focused on the spiritual work of prayer, teaching, and preaching to guide the body of Christ faithfully. However, this doesn't mean that they didn't take care of their personal business and their own families. What they were saying was that they recognized their spiritual responsibility to seek God's guidance to lead their people into maturity. It was not to spend their time serving meals in the church's soup kitchen.

We used to know a pastor who expected the men of his church to take care of his son, even when a church activity required the child's father to participate. This did not make for a happy son who was the only child there without his dad. Neither did it make the other children happy when it was supposed to be a special bonding time with their father.

Many times their fathers had to spend their time with the pastor's very needy child.

10. The early church engaged in constant prayer.

Did you notice the word *continually* in Acts 6:4? Somehow, today, without biblical validation, a special category called "intercessors" has been created. Even pastors use it as a title to describe those who have learned how to get into intercession. But biblically, it is not a special office or special gifting. While almost all church leadership agrees that prayer is foundational to every endeavor, only a precious few demonstrate any commitment to that belief in their own lives. Neither do they provide a room set aside in their buildings for nothing but prayer. I've visited and been a part of churches that have such a room. But inevitably, when the entire congregation meets all together, the "prayer room" is often used for a Sunday School class or for another purpose. The result is that if individual prayer ministry needs to take place during a church function, there is no place to do so.

One Sunday morning, two young girls stumbled into our church. One of them could hardly walk and the other was trying to help her. The night before, the afflicted girl had learned that her boyfriend was schooled and practiced in evil occultic arts. He'd demonstrated his skill in such a way that it almost scared the girl to death - literally. Here in America, it is not uncommon for many people to scoff at the dark arts as not being real. They choose to believe that it's just fun and games, something that Hollywood makes up to sell frightening movies, or is only practiced in other countries. But the night before, this girl saw a demonstration of the satanic. She was now needing deliverance,

> *Is there a place available in your building to pray during services?*

understanding, and the loving gospel of Jesus Christ. Though not a Christian herself, her friend felt that the kind of help she needed could be found only in a church. Ours just happened to be the nearest church.

I was called by the leadership to deal with the situation. Fortunately, our church had just rearranged some rooms and made a library that was not being used during the worship service. We had a quiet place to go so that God could intervene in this situation. Later, both girls walked out of the building delivered, and newborn babes in Christ. What a shame it would have been if there had not been a set-apart place for us to use while the rest of the congregation was participating in the worship service. Is there a place available in your building to pray during services that is away from distractions and interruptions? If not, why not?

Even leaders who believe in prayer can make compromises regarding this need. At the request of the head of a major, life-giving ministry, I was asked to prepare a prayer room for their staff. They cleaned out a small office in the center of the main building that was being used for storage. God gave us the funds, volunteer labor, and the necessary furniture. It turned out to be such an attractive room that within a year, the head of the ministry made it her office. There was, once again, nowhere on their large campus for quiet, uninterrupted prayer at any time of the day.

A word of caution: While it is nice to have a pleasant place to pray, even a dark, dingy, dirty hole of a room can be turned into a glorious place to host the Presence of the Lord. Paint and carpeting are not a requirement. The jail cell Paul and Silas were in is a prime example (Acts 16:25). When my children were still preschoolers, they would sometimes throw a blanket over a desk or chair to mimic my prayer closet. Find your personal prayer room, closet, or chair at home, and pray for such a place in your church facility.

11. Their prayer included:

- Visions – *Now the Lord spoke to Paul in the night by a vision, "Do not be afraid, but speak and do not keep silent"* (Acts 18:9).
- Dreams – *In a dream, in a vision of the night, when deep sleep falls upon men, while slumbering on their beds, then He opens the ears of men, and seals their instruction. In order to turn man from his deed,*

and conceal pride from man, He keeps back his soul from the Pit, and his life from perishing by the sword (Job 33:15-18). This was spoken by Job's fourth friend, Elihu, whom God did not reprimand.

- Angel messengers – *For there stood by me this night an angel of the God to whom I belong and whom I serve* (Acts 27:23).

12. Their prayers were in one accord without dissension, jealousy, or competition.

And when they had entered, they went up into the upper room . . . These all continued with one accord in prayer and supplication (Acts 1:13-14).

Acts 16:6-10 tells an interesting story. The apostle Paul, Silas, and Timothy were in the process of going through various cities, sharing the word of the Lord.

They were forbidden by the Holy Spirit to preach the word in Asia. After they had come to Mysia, they tried to go into Bithynia but the Spirit did not permit them (Acts 16:6-7).

And a vision appeared to Paul in the night. A man of Macedonia stood and pleaded with him, saying, "Come over to Macedonia and help us." Now after he had seen the vision, immediately we sought to go to Macedonia, concluding that the Lord had called us to preach the gospel to them (Acts 16:9-10).

Even though the vision came through Paul, the others were in agreement with him. There was no competition or jealousy among the disciples. God was the one on whom their minds were centered. Whoever He chose to speak through or give dreams or visions to was His business. I think they were just grateful that He was involved in their lives and spoke so much.

We are all called to a life of prayer. Therefore, we need to learn to distinguish between three voices:

1. Our own voice.
2. The voice of the Lord.
3. The voice of the enemy.

So I sought for a man among them who would make a wall, and stand in the gap before Me on behalf of the land, that I should not destroy it; but I found no one (Ezekiel 22:30).

He saw that there was no man, and wondered that there was no intercessor, therefore His own arm brought salvation for Him and His own righteousness, it sustained Him (Isaiah 59:16).

How many of us really want to fall into the category of being so selfish as to not be willing to intercede for our fellow man? We must not be hesitant because once in scripture God chose to speak through the *still, small voice*. The bulk of the time He spoke very loudly!

Wisdom calls aloud outside; she raises her voice in the open squares. She cries out in the chief concourses, at the openings of the gates in the city she speaks her words (Proverbs 1:20-21).

Wisdom is not a thing or something ethereal. Wisdom is a person: Father, Son, and Holy Spirit.

Our challenge is three-fold.

1. Be willing to receive and incorporate into our lives each of the 12 points listed above.
2. Experience "Enoch prayer" - walking and talking with God constantly.
3. Prepare ourselves and our churches to support prayer full time.

Moreover, as for me, far be it from me that I should sin against the Lord in ceasing to pray for you; but I will teach you the good and the right way (1 Samuel 12:23).

13

PROPHECY

The testimony of Jesus is the spirit of prophecy (Rev. 19:10).

The word *prophecy* is used in scripture in one of three different ways, which are often confused. Prophecy in its purest form is simply hearing God speak. When we give our lives to the Lord, confess our sins, and invite Him to take control of our lives, we receive the Holy Spirit who will then live inside of us.

Because of His presence, we can all hear God speak. Indeed, we have the responsibility of listening to Him. This ability to hear Him is not just for a chosen few. It is for anyone willing to learn how to distinguish His voice from their own. Sadly, I knew a pastor who said that he'd finally managed to get everyone to leave his church who thought they could hear God speak. Such theology does not line up with scripture. The result was that his church eventually had to close its doors.

There is the redemptive gift of prophecy. More about this later.

Finally, there is the office of prophet.

Like all the other gifts of the Spirit, the gift of prophecy cannot be bought, bargained for, or earned. It is a gift. Period. How far each of us gets into prophecy and the level to which God uses us in this gift depends on what we each do with 1 Corinthians 14:1. *Pursue love, and desire spiritual gifts, but especially that you may prophesy.*

Everyone can and should seek this gift, and anyone can be chosen of God to be a messenger for Him. But how the gift of prophecy is used, and if a person also fills the office of prophet, is strictly God's choice. It is His decision to designate them for speaking publicly, and it is His choice to set them in the public office of prophet.

Since the heart of prophecy is hearing God, sometimes the lines between prophet, teacher, apostle, etc., can become blurred. Some simple definitions:

- An apostle is a sent one who establishes and builds the church.
- The teacher explains and enforces biblical truth.
- The prophet is a messenger to the church.

"He or she is recognized as a divine channel of fresh revelation. This revelation is not extra-biblical revelation, but fresh light brought upon biblical truth." (Larry J. Randolph, *User Friendly Prophecy*, p. 21)

A word of prophecy will never contradict scripture.

PROPHECY DEFINED

Greek: "To speak in behalf of another; mouthpiece." Like a lawyer. A prophet or prophetess is a spokesperson for God to His people.

As each one has received a gift, minister it to one another as good stewards of the manifold grace of God. If anyone speaks, let him speak as the oracles of God. If anyone ministers, let him do it as with the ability which God supplies, that in all things God may be glorified through Jesus Christ, to whom belong the glory and the dominion forever and ever. Amen (1 Peter 4:10, 11).

Prophecy is simply God speaking through His people to His people. This gift is primarily given to those who have received the baptism of the Holy Spirit. This baptism releases the Holy Spirit, who dwells inside the believer, so that streams of living water can flow out from our lives. The baptism of the Holy Spirit is given for the purpose of being God's witnesses, of giving testimony about Jesus. Revelation 19:10 tells us that *the testimony of Jesus is the spirit of prophecy.*

The gift of prophecy is a resident anointing. It is something that comes out from within us. This is something people often don't understand. They think God just talks to "special" people. Or they pray and fast and wait for the Spirit to come upon them so they can prophesy. They don't understand the difference between how this gift was used before Jesus came, and how it was used after His resurrection.

Before Jesus, the gift of prophecy came upon a person. It came from outside themselves.

I have put My spirit upon Him (Isaiah 42:1).
The word of the Lord came to me (Ezekiel 6:1).
The spirit of the Lord God is upon Me (Isaiah 61:1).

Moses wanted all the people to be prophets but he thought in terms of the Spirit coming upon them. *Then Moses said to him, "Are you zealous for my sake? Oh, that all the Lord's people were prophets and that the Lord would put His Spirit upon them"* (Numbers 11:29).

Then the Lord came down in the cloud and spoke to him; and He took of the Spirit who was upon him and placed Him upon the seventy elders. And it came about that when the Spirit rested upon them, they prophesied. But they did not do it again (Numbers 11:25).

The gift of prophecy was dependent on an outside force at a particular time and place. It had little or nothing to do with their character, holy living, or personal righteousness. That is how it was possible for King Saul to be living in rebellion and still have the ability to prophesy.

When they came there to the hill, there was a group of prophets to meet him; then the Spirit of God came upon him (Saul), and he prophesied among them. And it happened, when all who knew him formerly saw that he indeed prophesied among the prophets, that the people said to one another, "What is this that has come upon the son of Kish? Is Saul also among the prophets?" (1 Samuel 10:10-11).

This same thing can happen today. A spirit of prophecy can fall on a congregation, and people who normally would not prophesy, find they can do so. However, God has more for us than just the spirit of prophecy.

God fulfilled Moses' desire for everyone to be a prophet when He sent Jesus. Jesus demonstrated the life of walking in the Spirit. Then He told His disciples, *It is to your advantage that I go away; for if I do not go away, the Helper will not come to you; but if I depart, I will send Him to you* (John 16:7).

He told them the Holy Spirit would come upon them (Acts 1:8). He had already told them that the *Spirit of truth…dwells with you and will be in you* (John 14:17).

When that happened, it set into play a whole new dynamic. The baptism of the Holy Spirit created an open channel for prophecy to flow – which happened when Peter preached his sermon on the day of Pentecost. Later, when Paul met the Christians in Ephesus, he met some disciples of John and asked, *Did you receive the Holy Spirit when you believed?* They said, "No." They submitted to water baptism, then Paul laid his hands on them and they spoke in tongues and prophesied (Acts 19:2-6). From that point on, we see how Holy Spirit baptism releases the Spirit resident within the believer.

Think on these verses:

- *They were all filled with the Holy Spirit...* (Acts 2:4).
- *Christ in you, the hope of glory* (Colossians 1:27).
- *...that He would grant you, according to the riches of His glory, to be strengthened with might through His Spirit in the inner man, that Christ may dwell in your hearts through faith...* (Ephesians 3:16-17).
- *Let the word of Christ dwell in you...* (Colossians 3:16).
- *But the anointing which you have received from Him abides in you...* (1 John 2:27).

The difference between before Jesus and after Jesus is that now the Holy Spirit is given freely to all of God's people to live inside of us.

Concerning the gift of prophecy . . . We are to seek the gift, not the ministry.

> *Now the Holy Spirit is given freely to all of God's people to live inside of us.*

There are diversities of gifts, but the same Spirit. There are differences of ministries, but the same Lord. And there are diversities of activities, but it is the same God who works all in all (1 Corinthians 12:4-6).

Pursue love, and desire spiritual gifts, but especially that you may prophesy (1 Corinthians 14:1).

It is from within that the ability and the gift of prophecy comes forth. That's why it is not only critical but necessary for the believer to learn to distinguish between his own voice and the Lord's voice. Prophecy will always come from an intimate walk with God. What used to happen just once in a while is now inside of every believer. Properly exercising it and using it for the benefit of others takes time, lots of discipline, humility, stumbling, falling, and sometimes a few cuts and bruises. We want God to speak to us in the natural, show us something we can see, touch, feel, or hear. And He often does

– through dreams, visions, an audible voice, angels, etc. But most of the time, it comes from within. And that is what makes using the gift of prophecy so scary. That's why we need to have the Word of God memorized in our hearts and minds.

Years ago, we became affiliated with a Spirit-filled church. As I got to know people, they would tell me what "God" had told them to do. I'd listen carefully, then ask them how they reconciled that direction with what the Bible said. And I'd quote a scripture that contradicted the guidance they'd received. Learn the Word. (The most valuable books you can have are a Bible and a concordance.)

"Old Testament prophecy is revelation received; whereas, much of New Testament prophecy is revelation perceived. The New Testament 'gift of prophecy' carries with it the privilege of interpreting the thought and intent of God's heart…We, as believers under the New Covenant, have a greater latitude of expression than did our Old Testament counterparts." (Larry J. Randolph, *User Friendly Prophecy*, p. 34)

When we speak a word of prophecy, it will come through our voice, with our way of expression, and in our language. Because of this, we must be careful not to discount a prophecy just because we don't like how it was delivered. As a degreed English teacher and writer by profession, I personally, have to be careful of this when the person giving the prophecy uses improper English grammar. That's why I say that the heart of any prophecy is the relationship between the vessel used and God Himself. Since He created us for fellowship with Himself, prophecy is at the core of the Christian life, which is walking and talking with God and being available for His use.

But the Lord said to me: "Do not say, 'I am a youth,' for you shall go to all to whom I send you, and whatever I command you, you shall speak. . . Then the Lord put forth His hand and touched my mouth, and the Lord said to me, "Behold, I have put My words in your mouth" (Jeremiah 1:7, 9).

And he (the seraphim) *touched my mouth with it* (the coal), *and said: "Behold, this has touched your lips; your iniquity is taken away, and your sin purged." Also I heard the voice of the Lord, saying: "Whom shall I send, and who will go for Us?"* (Isaiah 6:7, 8).

We are to not only be witnesses for the Lord, but we are also to be His voice to one another and to the world. *So Jesus said to them again, "Peace to you! As the Father has sent Me, I also send you"* (John 20:21).

God shares His secrets only with His friends, so our goal is to become His friend. How do we do this? By listening, communicating, spending time with Jesus; all the things you do to become someone's friend here on earth. There is one major difference between friendship with God and friendship with another person. God only calls us friends if we walk in obedience and submission to Him. As we walk in obedience, we can then prophesy, not because we're perfect, but because the Perfect Word is inside us. Prophecy is something that is developed over time by those who spend time with God.

THE CATEGORIES OF PROPHECY

There are ten categories of prophecy:

1. Edification
2. Exhortation
3. Comfort
4. Awaken God's people to hear His word and obey
5. Lead God's people into worship
6. Conviction
7. Impartation of something of value and substance
8. Know how to pray
9. Guidance or revelation
10. To foretell the future

Thus, it is easy to understand why all Christians are to seek this gift since we all are to *Sanctify the Lord God in your hearts, and always be ready to give a defense* (answer) *to everyone who asks you a reason for the hope that is in you, with meekness and fear* (1 Peter 3:15).

All can exercise this gift. *For you can all prophesy one by one, that all may learn and all may be encouraged* (1 Corinthians 14:31).

Even new believers. *When they heard this, they were baptized in the name of the Lord Jesus. And when Paul had laid hands on them, the Holy Spirit came upon them, and they spoke with tongues and prophesied* (Acts 19:5-6).

One year I took my five-year-old granddaughter with me to share the gospel with children at an event. A short time after she had led another child to the Lord, she looked at me and spoke a simple word of truth. At first, it sounded like something cute that a child would say. But later, as I thought about it, I realized that God had spoken a word of prophecy through her concerning my life.

The purpose of prophecy to an individual or group is:

1. <u>Edification</u> – to instruct or improve, to build, to establish, to confirm.

But he who prophesies speaks edification and exhortation and comfort to men (1 Corinthians 14:3).

Edification is like a defense attorney in a trial in which there are two people who address the sin of the defendant. The prosecuting attorney does so for the purpose of punishment. The defense attorney points out the sin for the purpose of saving him.

Biblical examples:

- God's promise to David about his name, his descendants, and the Messiah coming from his seed (1 Chronicles 17:7-15).
- Ananias edified Saul by telling him that God had chosen him to go to the Gentiles (Acts 9:10-18).
- Paul edified Timothy by reminding him of the prophecies previously made concerning him so that he could *wage the good warfare* (1 Timothy 1:18).
- Simeon edified Mary and Joseph when he blessed and prophesied over the child Jesus in the temple (Luke 2:27-33).

2. <u>Exhortation</u> – to encourage or urge earnestly by advice or warning, the act of crying out, wooing, calling near, a stirring up of things, and calling individuals and churches to a specific and concrete action.

But he who prophesies speaks edification and exhortation and comfort to men (1 Corinthians 14:3).

This gift is used to move people or a church forward in the direction they should go. My husband is an exhorter. It's just who he is. Consequently, if he doesn't have people around himself to exhort, he'll exhort our cats, chickens, and trees. When he has a prophecy for someone, it comes out as an exhortation.

Biblical examples:

- *Now Judas and Silas, themselves being prophets also, exhorted and strengthened the brethren with many words* (Acts 15:32).
- *Preach the word! Be ready in season and out of season. Convince, rebuke, exhort, with all longsuffering and teaching* (2 Timothy 4:2).
- *When he came and had seen the grace of God, he was glad, and encouraged them all that with purpose of heart they should continue with the Lord* (Acts 11:23).

- *Barnabas and Paul strengthening the souls of the disciples, exhorting them to continue in the faith, and saying, We must through many tribulations, enter the kingdom of God* (Acts 14:22). They then appointed elders in every church in order to move the church forward.
- *Therefore, I exhort first of all that supplications, prayers, intercessions, and giving of thanks be made for all men* (1 Timothy 2:1).
- *Likewise, exhort the young men to be sober-minded* (Titus 2:6).

3. <u>Comfort</u> – to comfort or cheer, to come alongside, to strengthen and reinforce.

But he who prophesies speaks edification and exhortation and comfort to men (1 Corinthians 14:3).

Psalm 78 is a seventy-two verse Psalm reminding the people of all the ways God has helped them in the past, giving them comfort for the present time. Change and advancement often come with great turmoil or "birth pangs." Comfort is needed not to provide pity or to encourage self-pity, but is always offered so that the afflicted can focus on the purpose beyond the turmoil, on the hope set before them.

"The prophet makes sense of turmoil or suffering, gives it purpose and therefore settles the hearts of God's people. This is consolation." (R. Loren Sandford, *Understanding Prophetic People*, p. 78)

Biblical examples:

- *For the Lord will comfort Zion, He will comfort all her waste places* (Isaiah 51:3a).
- *The Spirit of the Lord God is upon Me, because the Lord has anointed Me to preach good tidings to the poor; He has sent Me to heal the brokenhearted, to proclaim liberty to the captives, and the opening of the prison to those who are bound; to proclaim the acceptable year of the Lord, and the day of vengeance of our God; to comfort all who mourn* (Isaiah 61:1-2).

- *Blessed be the God and Father of our Lord Jesus Christ, the Father of mercies and God of all comfort who comforts us in all our tribulation, that we may be able to comfort those who are in any trouble, with the comfort with which we ourselves are comforted by God* (2 Corinthians 1:3-4). Did you notice that comfort or some form of the word is repeated five times in just these two verses?
- *Therefore comfort each other and edify one another, just as you also are doing* (1 Thessalonians 5:11).
- *Now we exhort you brethren, warn those who are unruly, comfort the fainthearted, uphold the weak, be patient with all* (1 Thessalonians 5:14). Have you ever visited someone sick at home or in the hospital? Did you try to comfort them? If so, you operated in the ministry of prophecy.
- *Nevertheless God, who comforts the downcast, comforted us by the coming of Titus* (2 Corinthians 7:6). You see here that the act of sending Titus to Paul was a prophetic act. And comfort imparts mercy.
- *For judgment is without mercy to the one who has shown no mercy. Mercy triumphs over judgment* (James 2:13).
- *Speak comfort to Jerusalem, and cry out to her, that her warfare is ended, that her iniquity is pardoned; for she has received from the Lord's hand double for all her sins* (Isaiah 40:2).
- *Or do you despise the riches of His goodness, forbearance, and longsuffering, not knowing that the goodness of God leads you to repentance?* (Romans 2:4).

4. Awaken God's people to hear His word and obey

Then the Spirit entered me when He spoke to me, and set me on my feet; and I heard Him who spoke to me. And He said to me; "Son of man, I am sending you to the children of Israel, to a rebellious nation that has rebelled against Me; they and their fathers have transgressed against Me to this very day. For they are impudent and stubborn children. I am sending you to them, and you shall say to them, 'Thus says the Lord God'" (Ezekiel 2:2-4).

Moreover He said to me: "Son of man, receive into your heart all My words that I speak to you, and hear with your ears And go, get to the captives, to the children of your people, and speak to them and tell them, 'Thus says the Lord God,' whether they hear, or whether they refuse" (Ezekiel 3:10, 11).

And to the angel (messenger) of the church in Sardis, write, "These things says He who has the seven Spirits of God and the seven stars; I know your works, that you have a name that you are alive, but you are dead. Be watchful, and strengthen the things which remain, that are ready to die, for I have not found your works perfect before God. Remember, therefore how you have received and heard; hold fast and repent. Therefore if you will not watch, I will come upon you as a thief, and you will not know what hour I will come upon you" (Revelation 3:1-3).

Notice some of the specific words used here. When God talks to the prophet, He uses words like listen or hear, receive or take, go, speak, say. When the prophet then takes the word of God and speaks to the people, he uses words like wake up or be watchful, strengthen, remember, hold fast, repent. It is also worth noting that the recipients of the prophetic word could have heard the word themselves, but they did not.

A prophetic word is characterized by the Holy Spirit's action both in the speaker and the hearer. Something happens. God's word is power and authority. Ezekiel's valley of dry bones came together at the spoken word of prophecy. Pharaoh hardened his heart when Moses spoke the words of prophecy. The power of God is brought into action in some way.

As for them, whether they hear or whether they refuse – for they are a rebellious house – yet they will know that a prophet has been among them (Ezekiel 2:5).

One year my husband and I made an appointment to talk to our pastor about a decision he was about to make that we knew from experience would divide the church. In the process of our talk, I delivered a strong prophetic word to him. He listened, changed his mind, and was able to live out his calling with honor. Years later and with the backing of my husband, I gave a prophetic teaching to another pastor. He was obviously convicted and about to repent. But sadly, we watched him slowly talk himself out of what God had spoken to him. Within a week, he no longer had a church. We must each recognize when God speaks to us through another, and pay attention to what He directs.

5. Lead God's people into worship

Moreover, David and the captains of the army separated for the service some of the sons of Asaph, of Heman, and of Jeduthun, who should prophesy with harps, stringed instruments and cymbals (1 Chronicles 25:1, 3).

Worship was often with musical accompaniment. *Sing to the Lord with thanksgiving; sing praises on the harp to our God* (Psalm 147:7).

At an area-wide prayer gathering, we participate in every month, there is a young man who truly exemplifies prophesying as he helps lead worship. He is a drummer. One day the Lord gave me the interpretation of how he was drumming. I shared it with the others and they recognized it also. Our prayer time became aligned with his prophetic drumming.

Examples of prophetic songs are found in Psalm 24; 29; 98; 100; 107. This is sometimes called inspirational prophecy, which is concerned more with the response of the hearers than in giving direction or communication.

6. Conviction

If all prophesy, and an unbeliever or an uninformed person comes in, he is convinced by all, he is convicted by all. And thus the secrets of his heart are revealed; and so, falling down on his face, he will worship God and report that God is truly among you (1 Corinthians 14:24-25).

If we feel we are to give a prophetic word for the purpose of conviction, we're in trouble. Conviction is the job of the Holy Spirit. Our job is to be sure we're right and that our hearts are pure. When I've given a word of prophecy, my intent or purpose usually is to teach or inform. How the Holy Spirit uses the prophecy and how the person receives it is not my responsibility. My job is to simply be obedient to speak what God gives me.

A convicting word of prophecy gives the person a chance to humble himself and repent. Most of the time, if he or she won't repent, they will respond in anger so the prophet must be prepared to receive the anger and not respond in kind. Some teachers of prophecy say this aspect of prophecy should be done only by the mature prophet. I don't believe that simply because I've seen young ones - like my 5-year-old granddaughter - be used this way. God simply uses the available and the pure in heart.

I believe that prophetic words of correction or rebuke should only be used as a last resort, and only under the guidelines of being cleaned out, 'fessed up, and with accountability, after being thoroughly washed in tears. Its purpose is not to get something off your chest; it's to confront sin, call for change, and offer hope. It's not to wound the other person. It is for the purpose of healing.

7. Impartation of something of value and substance

Biblical Examples:

- Timothy was imparted a gift by prophetic utterance that Paul told him not to neglect. *Do not neglect the gift that is in you, which was given to you by prophecy with the laying on of the hands of the eldership* (1 Timothy 4:14).
- Jacob gave his sons and Joseph's children prophetic blessings before his death (Genesis 48-49).

- Moses laid hands on Joshua, before the people, and spoke the prophetic word of authority over him as instructed by the Lord (Numbers 27:18-23).
- *And when He had called His twelve disciples to Him, He gave them power over unclean spirits, to cast them out, and to heal all kinds of sickness and all kinds of disease* (Matthew 10:1).

This requires spiritual stamina and, if the impartation is not to be from your soul, it requires spiritual maturity. Only what has been put in us by the Holy Spirit is worth imparting to others. Again, not for the novice in the prophetic. Many people want prayer for the impartation of a gift or talent so they don't have to work for it. Such a desire is very soulish. Impartation, as an aspect of prophecy, is from spirit to spirit.

8. Know how to pray

Many Old Testament prophets who were called on to pray and intercede for people had to first go to God for instruction as to how to pray.

For we do not know what we should pray for as we ought (Romans 8:26).

"When answers to prayer and the release of power depend upon the accuracy of our words, then we have left the realm of prayer and entered into magic . . . It is, however important to discern the will of God to the best of our ability and to align ourselves with it." (R. Loren Sandford, *Understanding Prophetic People*, p. 87)

There is nothing wrong with working to get the words right and making sure that everyone in a prayer group understands what is to be prayed for. In fact, this is commendable so that everyone is united in understanding. But when we take this effort to the extreme, that's when it can slip into the realm of magic or witchcraft.

Now this is the confidence that we have in Him, that if we ask anything according to His will, He hears us (1 John 5:14).

"When praying seems blocked and the connection broken, the prophetic role is to discern why." (R. Loren Sandford, *Understanding Prophetic People*, p. 89)

Once during prayer with a strategic-level prayer group, we discerned that our prayers were being blocked. We sought the Lord as to why. He showed us that a visitor, who'd come that day, wanted to control the group. Before the meeting began, I had met and warned her that this was a group that operated in a high level of warfare and that if any of us were out of line, or not up to the task, God had told us that our secret sins would be made known publically. I showed her where she could go to get herself ready if she needed to. Unfortunately, she ignored this, joined the group, and proceeded to try to derail the prayer time and the purpose God had for us that day. The result was that her sins were made public. Shamed and angry, she stormed out of the meeting and left the church altogether. We later learned that she'd tried to insert herself into leadership in every ministry within this large church. Fortunately, the prayer group was her last effort because God revealed the motives of her heart.

9. Guidance or revelation

It was by revelation He made known to me the mystery (as I have briefly written already, by which, when you read, you may understand my knowledge in the mystery of Christ), which in other ages was not made known to the sons of men, as it has now been revealed by the Spirit to His holy apostles and prophets (Ephesians 3:3-5).

Biblical examples:

- Peter received revelation through a vision that the Gentiles were not to be considered unclean (Acts 10:10-16).
- Paul received the prophecy about persecution awaiting him if he went to Jerusalem (Acts 21:4, 10-11). This is an example of not understanding a vision or word until a particular circumstance happens.

- God instructed Hosea to take a harlot for his wife (Hosea 1:2-3).
- Samuel gave Saul prophetic guidance about the result of his disobedience in not killing Agag and destroying all that they had (1 Samuel 15:28-33).
- The Holy Spirit told Philip to take a particular road, then, once he got there, He told him to speak to the Ethiopian eunuch in the chariot (Acts 8:26-40). This is an example of God giving step-by-step instructions. We never get away from needing to trust when we don't know what God is leading us into. Our job is to trust and obey step by step as Philip did.

Prophetic guidance can be general or specific. It can be very helpful to people or churches, but it must be done only with caution and typically not by the beginner. If we are wrong about the direction we give, we bear the responsibility and judgment that comes if we lead someone down the wrong path. I had a dear friend whom I'd discipled after she left a cult she had been a part of for many years. Sadly, she was eventually diagnosed with bone marrow cancer. Through much prayer, deliverance, and following the directions of a specialist, her healing was progressing. She got engaged and was making plans for the rest of her life. Finally, the doctor told her that she needed a bone marrow transplant. However, a woman, claiming to be a prophetess, told her that she didn't need such surgery and that she was healed. So, without checking out the history of this "prophetess," she canceled the surgery. A short time later, my friend died. It wasn't until a few years later that I learned why she didn't go through with the transplant. I'd also learned more about the lady "prophet" whom I'd only met once. She was a woman with a reputation for controlling people, claiming the prophetic gift, and manipulating people out of their money. When she would wear out her welcome in a church, she'd move on to another congregation.

Fortunately, I learned her true nature at the same time that she found out how to contact me. Desperate for another church to infiltrate, she wanted me to tell her where my church was located. I did not follow through and informed my pastor in case she tried to get a foothold in our fellowship. God is good about protecting us, using us to protect others, and giving guidance about everything that concerns us if we listen, trust and obey.

10. To foretell the future

Surely the Lord God does nothing, unless He reveals His secret to His servants the prophets (Amos 3:7).

Biblical examples:

- The prophecy of Agabus to Paul (Acts 21:8-11).
- Much of Daniel, Ezekiel, Isaiah, Revelation, etc.
- Agabus prophesied a great famine throughout all the world (Acts 11:27, 28).
- Jeremiah prophesied that the vessels in the house of the Lord would not be brought back from Babylon (Jeremiah 28:15-29:10).

Historical reports tell us that Christians in Jerusalem moved to Pella before Titus sacked the city because they believed Jesus' prophecy *when you see Jerusalem surrounded by armies* (Luke 21:20).

In the fall of 1975, during the civil war in Lebanon, a prophecy warned Christians in Beirut to leave their homes and live for a while in the U.S. Shortly after they left, their building was bombed.

The U.S. World Trade Center was destroyed by two airplanes crashing into its towers on September 11, 2001. The prayer group I was a part of in Dallas, Texas had been forewarned by the Holy Spirit that something major was going to happen in the nation. We didn't know what exactly, but we were prepared within our spirits. Then when the tragedy occurred, we all gasped, but immediately took a deep breath, and said, "Oh, so this is what God was preparing us for." Without having to overcome shock and dismay, we were able to be used by the Lord to comfort others.

Months later, three women from two different countries in Southeast Asia, found their way to our prayer group. Much earlier, the leader had been given a vision of the towers coming down. Gathering her two prayer partners, they traveled to the United States to warn the Body of Christ. A number of churches would not receive them. Others didn't believe them. But there was an Asian-American church in the New York City area that both received them, and believed them. Quite a few members of this particular church worked in the World Trade Center. But not one of them died or was hurt when the tragedy happened. In fact, many of them did not go to work that day. The people in this church followed the command, *Believe His prophets, and so you shall be blessed* (2 Chronicles 20:20).

JUDGING PROPHECY

Measures by which prophecy must be judged are:

1. <u>It will be fulfilled.</u>

When a prophet speaks in the name of the Lord, if the thing does not happen or come to pass, that is the thing which the Lord has not spoken; the prophet has spoken it presumptuously; you shall not be afraid of him (Deuteronomy 18:22).

Fulfillment must take into consideration any and all "ifs" God may put in. Many prophecies carry a condition that must be met before the prophecy can be fulfilled. Thus, Jonah was not a false prophet. But even if it comes true, if it or the person giving it leads you away from God, it is not from the Lord.

If there arises among you a prophet or a dreamer of dreams, and he gives you a sign or a wonder, and the sign or the wonder comes to pass, of which he spoke to you, saying, 'Let us go after other gods' – which you have not known – 'and let us serve them,' you shall not listen to the words of that prophet or that dreamer of dreams, for the Lord your God is testing you to know whether you love the Lord your God with all your heart and with all your soul. You shall walk after the Lord your God and fear Him, and keep His commandments and obey His voice; you shall serve Him and hold fast to Him (Deuteronomy 13:1-4).

2. <u>It will agree with scripture; it can be tested</u>.

Every word of God is pure, He is a shield to those who put their trust in Him" (Proverbs 30:5).

As for God, His way is perfect; the word of the Lord is proven; He is a shield to all who trust in Him (2 Samuel 22:31).

All Scripture is given by inspiration of God, and is profitable for doctrine, for reproof, for correction, for instruction in righteousness (2 Timothy 3:16).

3. <u>Prophecy will witness or be confirmed by your spirit</u>.

But the Holy Spirit also witnesses to us; for after He had said before, 'This is the covenant that I will make with them after those days, says the Lord: I will put My laws into their hearts, and in their minds I will write them' (Hebrews 10:15-16).

God doesn't sneak up on us and surprise us if we are continually attuned to Him. He prepares the ground for the seed of truth before planting. We respond in agreement, in anger, or dismiss it, depending on our attitude.

As for them, whether they hear or whether they refuse – for they are a rebellious house – yet they will know that a prophet has been among them (Ezekiel 2:5).

4. <u>The fruit of the Spirit will be obvious in the life of the person prophesying.</u>

Not a novice, lest being puffed up with pride he fall into the same condemnation as the devil (1 Timothy 3:5).

You will know them by their fruits (Matthew 7:16).

Therefore, by their fruits, you will know them (Matthew 7:20).

His or her home life will be in order, bills paid, etc. In other words, they will be people of integrity. Integrity means you are the same on the inside as you are on the outside. This means that your mouth and your behavior at home are the same as when you are in public. And your thought-life is the same as your actions. We once knew a man who enjoyed lining up places to speak and give personal prophecies. But over time, I realized that his prophecies often didn't come true. Then we discovered that his home life wasn't in order. In fact, it was so out of order that his wife left him, and today they are divorced.

5. <u>The spirit of the prophet will be Jesus.</u>

For the testimony of Jesus is the spirit of prophecy (Revelation 19:10).

However, when He, the Spirit of truth, has come, He will guide you into all truth; for He will not speak on His own authority but whatever He hears He will speak; and He will tell you things to come. He will glorify Me, for He will take of what is Mine and declare it to you (John 16:13, 14).

The motivation for giving a prophetic word, even if it is one of judgment, will be love.

By this you know the Spirit of God: Every spirit that confesses that Jesus Christ has come in the flesh is of God...God is love, and he who abides in love abides in God, and God in him (1 John 4:2, 16).

For you, brethren, have been called to liberty; only do not use liberty as an opportunity for the flesh, but through love serve one another (Galatians 5:13).

Now the purpose of the commandment is love from a pure heart, from a good conscience, and from sincere faith (1 Timothy 1:5).

By this all will know that you are My disciples, if you have love for one another (John 13:35).

6. <u>It won't be given in a corner or done in a covert way.</u>

He who speaks in a tongue edifies himself, but he who prophesies edifies the church (1 Corinthians 14:4).

It is judged by the giver before he gives it.

Beloved, do not believe every spirit, but test the spirits, whether they are of God; because many false prophets have gone out into the world (1 John 4:1).

It is to be judged by other prophets after he gives it.

Let two or three prophets speak, and let the others judge (1 Corinthians 14:29).

7. <u>It may include the "revelation gifts" – word of wisdom, word of knowledge, discerning of spirits. These four gifts often overlap each other.</u>

For to one is given the word of wisdom through the Spirit, to another the word of knowledge through the same Spirit, to another faith by the same Spirit, to another gifts of healings by the same Spirit, to another the working of miracles, to another prophecy, to another discerning of spirits, to another different kinds of tongues, to another the interpretation of tongues (1 Corinthians 12:8-10).

If a particular prophecy is delivered that meets all of the above guidelines except #4 (the fruit of the Spirit growing in the life of the one giving a prophecy), it would be safe to conclude that person is out of tune with the Lord or doesn't know the whole situation.

When a prophecy is given to a group and the giver meets all the criteria listed above but it doesn't witness to your spirit, it is possible the particular prophecy is for an individual in the group, and not you. In these cases, your responsibility is to pray for the recipient to have an open heart. You must always be aware that the person needing the open heart could be yourself. We all have blind spots. Be careful not to get into a judgmental attitude. We need to recognize that anyone who prophesies does so with the level of faith, the knowledge, and the understanding of the gift that they have at that particular time.

We then, who are strong, ought to bear with the weaknesses of the weak, and not to please ourselves. Let each of us please his neighbor for his good, leading to edification. For even Christ did not please Himself (Romans 15:1-3).

In other words, we must allow for one another's mistakes and immaturity.

A SHORT EXPLANATION OF THE GIFTS OF THE SPIRIT

Revelation Gifts

Word of wisdom = Divine application of God's will for a person or situation

Word of knowledge = Knowing something that you have no way of knowing in the natural even though other people may know it. A man spoke over me one time thinking he was giving me a prophecy of the kingdom work I would be doing in the future. But God was actually giving him a word of knowledge because he was telling what work God had me doing in the past.

Discernment of spirits = Recognizing the demonic. Notice that this type of discernment is of demonic spirits, not the soulish discernment of another's heart attitude. "Regular" discernment is distinguishing between black and white, right and wrong. Discernment can be gained through experience, the study of personalities, body language, etc. But that kind of discernment is not a Gift of the Spirit. This is why Discernment of Spirits, as given in 1 Corinthians 12:8-10, is considered one of the "Revelation gifts" along with words of wisdom and knowledge. It is not mind-reading or putting your feelings on someone else.

Power Gifts
Working of miracles
Healing
Faith

Utterance Gifts
Tongues
Interpretation of tongues
Prophecy

LEVELS OF THE PROPHETIC

The use of the prophetic gift depends upon calling, maturity, personality, and ministry. In recent years, recognized prophets have begun to distinguish four levels of the prophetic.

The spirit of prophecy. This is when the anointing of the Holy Spirit falls on a group of people making it possible for non-prophetic people to prophesy. This often happens in prayer groups and worship gatherings. My husband and I attended a conference at the International House of Prayer in Kansas City, Kansas one year. After an hour of worship, the spirit of prophecy fell on the large gathering such that it seemed like everyone was prophesying to everyone else. Even my husband, who previously had said he didn't receive prophecies, was giving people words from the Lord, and they were being confirmed. It was such an encouragement to him that since then, when God gives him a word for another person, he is comfortable giving it.

The gift of prophecy. This is given to fewer people, even though all believers are told to seek it. This is a gift planted within the person that can be used anytime, anywhere, dependent only on how developed in its use they are.

The prophetic mantle. This is stronger in commitment. It is a lifestyle devoted to the prophetic. It permeates every aspect of your life.

The office of prophet. This is a sovereign calling on people who have had extensive experience in hearing God's voice. It is also a governmental office in the church. It will include all the aspects of prophecy. Even when it is not recognized formally, it is the only level where a person has the authority to direct or correct an entire body of believers.

Examples of people with the gift of prophecy and the ministry of prophet are as follows:

GIFT: Amos was a herdsman and fig picker.

GIFT: Isaiah's wife was a prophetess, but...

MINISTRY: God used Isaiah in the ministry to speak to Israel. At the same time...

GIFT: Micah was a farmer who prophesied at the same time as Isaiah. He prophesied about Jesus' birth. Isaiah prophesied about Jesus' death.

GIFT: Jeremiah was a prophet with the ministry of a priest.

MINISTRY: Ezekiel was a priest with the ministry of prophet.

GIFT: Phillip's daughters had the gift but…

MINISTRY: Agabus was given the ministry, in the presence of Philip's daughters. He also prophesied the coming famine.

My husband, Gary, has the gift of exhortation. His ministry is helps or service. But he often operates in the gift of prophecy, whereas I carry the prophetic mantle. God sovereignly placed me in the office of prophet for a specific body of believers for several years, but it was not a permanent position.

First Corinthians 12:4-7 tells us there are not only different gifts, but different administrations and operations of those gifts. This gives the Lord a lot of variety and choices to mix and match gifts, ministries, and personalities. A good example is the contrast between Haggai and Zechariah. Both were prophets, but how they used their gift and fulfilled their ministries was different.

HAGGAI	ZECHARIAH
1. Used sermons	1. Used sermons
2. Was an exhorter	2. Was an encourager
3. Spoke on the spur of the moment with rebuke	3. Spoke from the heart with restoration
4. Concerned with the present: Finish the temple! Take part!	4. Concerned with the future: Messiah is coming! Take heart!

MARKS OF THE PROPHETIC GIFT

- They are called.
- They are aware of history.
- They appreciate and use symbolism and allegories.
- They are intercessors.
- They enjoy silence.
- They are watchmen on the walls, seeing what the Lord is going

to do in the future and proclaiming it to prepare the people. Even if the warning is negative, it comes in a protective mode.

- They are burden bearers. (Not all burden bearers are prophetic, but all prophetic people are burden bearers.) *
- They are constantly confronted by God.
- They have the "gift" of weakness.*
- They must live the life of the cross more deeply than others, often resulting in seasons of heaviness.*
- Spiritual warfare is never the focus. "Look deep into the writings of the biblical prophets and you will find tender hearts, broken for God, and broken for Israel. They were lovers first, and warriors only when they had to be" (R. Loren Sandford, *Understanding Prophetic People*, p. 70).
- They get dreams and visions.
- They are very clear that the word is from God, but can't tell you how they know.
- They use words and show, by their actions, that they believe the word.
- They are public speakers, and often, writers.
- They carry with them, at all times, authority and presence that validates itself with most, but which others can choose to be intimidated by.*

  "Even when pride is absent, and humility has become an established element of character, the authority radiating from a prophet can elicit accusations of arrogance." (R. Loren Sandford, *Understanding Prophetic People*, p. 105)

  A good example of this is Aaron and Miriam when they accused Moses in Numbers 12:2.

- They have more than their share of rejection, and often become the scapegoat.*

  It is important to note, however, that when the prophet suffers, it is because of their standing for the word and work of the Lord. For a time, I knew a lady who decided she had a prophetic gift simply because she'd suffered so much in her life.

However, anyone who knew her and her past, knew that much of her suffering had to do with her own poor, even unbiblical, choices.

- They may be a prophet with local, national, or global responsibility and must be careful to remain in the sphere God has given them. These spheres can grow but they can also decrease. For example, generally speaking, I am a national governmental intercessor. God has made it very clear that even though it is within my state and nation, specific involvement in the county that borders ours, which is only two miles away from my house, is not within my scope of responsibility at this time. Naturally, I pray for them but I am not to become overly involved in the affairs of that county though I am often invited to do so. As always, prophets must know the boundaries that God has set for them and then stay within those boundaries.
- They ask questions about life and faith that do not seem to matter to others.*
- They look for answers in places others never seem to consider and seek the deep meaning of things others seem to accept at face value.*
- They are incapable of settling for anything that strikes them as shallow.*
- They are often born with a crushing sense of destiny and live under a sense of urgency.*
- They are lost without the support of others' prayers for protection and effectiveness in ministry.*

In 1998 my husband and I were asked to be a part of an eight-person team that traveled to India. We were there to dedicate a church building that the ladies of our church had raised money to construct. Additionally, we were there, with our pastor, to determine what type of ministry our church might establish there. I knew God wanted me to go, but I also knew, at that time, I was not physically capable of such an arduous journey. Nevertheless, I said, "yes," then told the Lord in all sincerity,

"Lord, I don't care if I die in India or not. But it would really ruin the trip for the others if I did, so please take care of that." I was not flippant or presumptuous. Instead, I began to recruit people who would commit to pray for me specifically. By the time we boarded our airplane, 75 people had made such a commitment. Some prayed daily; some prayed whenever they thought about me, and one person even fasted one meal a day for me the entire time we were gone. In spite of my physical issues, I was the only team member who did not get sick either while we were in India or after returning home. In fact, I didn't even have jet lag going or coming! To this day, as President of Vawtermark Ministries, Inc., I maintain monthly communication with a group of people who are committed to praying for me. I believe this should be the norm for anyone in ministry whether they have a prophetic mantle, carry the office, or not. We need the support of others.

- They are forerunners; often one step ahead of the rest of the Body of Christ.*

This last point is why churches are now beginning to realize that God knew what He was doing when He set apostles and prophets first in the listing of spiritual gifts for the church.

And God has appointed these in the church: first apostles, second prophets, third teachers, after that miracles, then gifts of healings, helps, administrations, varieties of tongues (1 Corinthians 12:28).

And He Himself gave some to be apostles, some prophets, some evangelists, and some pastors and teachers, for the equipping of the saints for the work of ministry, for the edifying of the body of Christ, till we all come to the unity of the faith and of the knowledge of the Son of God, to a perfect man, to the measure of the stature of the fullness of Christ (Ephesians 4:11-13).

---

* Concepts taught in the book, *Understanding Prophetic People*, by R. Loren Sandford.

"In this passage, Paul painted a picture of an archway with apostles and prophets at the bases of the arch. As living stones, we form the curving walls of the arch, while Jesus as the cornerstone at the apex nevertheless bears the weight of the arches. Everything points upward to Him, and in Him, it all holds together. But essential to the structure is a functioning foundational prophetic ministry. Prophetic ministry restores a measure of integrity, guidance, and preparation to the Church. It also restores the foundation God intended," says R. Loren Sandford on page 45 of his book, *Understanding Prophetic People*. (Since this is obviously true, what is the pastor? A pastor is the medic, binding up the wounds of the flock and taking care of them.)

HOW TO GROW IN THE GIFT OF PROPHECY

As with the other gifts of the Spirit, but even more so with the gift of prophecy, we must have a purpose for seeking it, growing in it, and using it. Without a purpose, we don't know what we're aiming for, and therefore, we might end up with what we don't want. When looking for your purpose, search the scriptures. Here are some passages that will steer us in the right direction.

- *Encourage one another daily, while it is called "Today," lest any of you be hardened through the deceitfulness of sin* (Hebrews 3:13).
- *Therefore comfort each other and edify* (build one another up) *one another* (1 Thessalonians 5:11).
- *Even so you, since you are zealous for spiritual gifts, let it be for the edification* (building up) *of the church that you seek to excel* (1 Corinthians 14:12).
- *Speaking the truth in love may grow up in all things into Him who is the head – Christ – from whom the whole body, joined and knit together by what every joint supplies, according to the effective working by which every part does its share, causes growth of the body for the edifying of itself in love* (Ephesians 4:15-16).

- *You also, as living stones, are being built up a spiritual house, a holy priesthood, to offer up spiritual sacrifices acceptable to God through Jesus Christ* (1 Peter 2:5).
- *A word fitly spoken is like apples of gold in settings of silver* (Proverbs 25:11).

When we "discern" something negative about someone, it is because of one of three reasons;

1. We've discerned a spirit from which they need to be delivered.
2. We've received a word of knowledge.
3. Something in their personality agitates something in ours.

Most of the time our "discernment" is for the third reason and we have the three fingers pointing back at ourselves. I believe that, for most of us, this third point is what keeps us from receiving one another with pure love. And when we don't want to or are unable to see as God sees and change ourselves, we call it discernment about the other person. I know a man who has "discerned" an undercurrent of anger in another man in his church. He is right, but he is not acknowledging a similar undercurrent of anger in himself.

Often what bothers us in someone else is actually the very thing we either consciously or subconsciously dislike in ourselves. Years ago, a lady in a small group we were leading had a word of "prophecy" for another lady in the group. But it was actually a word God had given her about herself that she didn't want to acknowledge, so she passed it off to another. And it didn't fit the other lady at all.

We must be careful not to prophesy out of our feelings. If we're angry with a person or church, whatever we say may be right, but it will come out angry and not be received. If we're touched by their hurt, it can come out mushy. We must learn to lay aside our own emotions and express the emotions of God, with His heart and His attitude. Keep in mind that God does a lot of crying, but when He does, it's not mushy. It merely shows His broken heart over our sins or trials.

To grow, we need not think too highly of ourselves or presume we are at a place spiritually that we're not. If we don't, we'll end up running ahead of the Holy Spirit. Worse still, we run ahead of our gifting, and we end up operating in the flesh. This can harm the person we're trying to help as well as ourselves. We can't give what we don't have. We must minister with the level of faith that we have, not someone else's. *Do you see a man wise in his own eyes? There is more hope for a fool than for him* (Proverbs 26:12).

If you have the gift of prophecy or seek it, you will become very sensitive to spiritual impulses of all kinds. Hence the need to always check what you hear with the word of God. Scripture advises us to judge everything carefully, including all prophetic utterances.

Beloved, do not believe every spirit, but test the spirits, whether they are of God; because many false prophets have gone out into the world (1 John 4:1).

Do not despise prophecies. Test all things; hold fast what is good (1 Thessalonians 5:20,21).

We need to remain teachable to learn from those who are more advanced in the gift of prophecy than ourselves. Be willing to start at the bottom and exercise patience. This will take time, trial, endurance, and suffering. Look at Joseph, Moses, Joshua, David. They all started at the bottom until they became content to stay there. Then, in God's timing, they were promoted.

> *We need to remain teachable.*

He who is faithful in what is least is faithful also in much (Luke 16:10).

God increases faith to the faithful.

We need to stop seeking a prophetic word for ourselves and become a channel to give a word to others.

> God increases faith to the faithful.

The Son of Man did not come to be served, but to serve (Matthew 20:28).

It is more blessed to give than to receive (Acts 20:35).

We must walk in obedience and leave the results to God.

We need to seek God as to what to do with the gift He's given us, and then obey what He says.

We must remain pure in regard to things of the flesh such as violence, sexual perversion, the occult. The counterfeit gift of prophecy is out there and it will grab us if we allow an opening. A minister once asked me to pray for him that he would be able to see angels. After I did, he told me that as I prayed, God spoke to his heart, telling him He would not allow him to see angels yet because he was not sufficiently free from all the pornography he'd been into before becoming a Christian. Another time, a woman asked me to pray for her to see angels. When I did, God gave her a vision of a circle with an angel's face in the circle. Across the angel's face was a diagonal line much like a road sign that alerts people not to enter a road. She immediately knew why she was seeing such a vision. She said that it was because of all the occult she'd practiced before becoming a Christian.

We must endure. This endurance includes the enduring of time, circumstance, other people, accusations, and misunderstandings. The true prophet will have to deal with a lot of misunderstandings. In fact, according to Loren Sandford, "For a prophetic person, training involves depths of crushing and breaking that seem incomprehensible to the average Christian. . . (There is) the pressure of the constant seasons of crucifixion required to produce the character adjustments that are so essential to the calling." (*Understanding Prophetic People*, p. 21)

We must not draw attention to our gifting or take credit for what we receive. No bragging. God tells His secrets to people He can trust. We must prophesy with integrity. If we have to tell people we have the gift of prophecy to get them to listen to us, or get someone else to tell them, then we probably don't have the gift.

We must have patience. In time, *a man's gift makes room for him, and brings him before great men* (Proverbs 18:16). It takes time. *But we all, with unveiled face, beholding as in a mirror the glory of the Lord, are being transformed into the same image from glory to glory, just as by the Spirit of the Lord* (1 Corinthians 3:18).

We must be willing to be in submission to God, to those whom God has made us accountable, and to our peers. *Submitting to one another in the fear of God* (Ephesians 5:21).

Agabus delivered his prophecy to Paul but stopped short of commanding him, thus allowing him to make his own decision. We must also do this with a good attitude. A right attitude is necessary for us to work in harmony with what God is doing in the larger body of Christ and protect our gift from becoming contaminated. According to Sandford, "Imbalance and delusion too often gain entry through a window of insecurity. Prophetic self-importance serves to cover up unresolved pain. The contemporary prophetic word can never be exempt from correction and testing." (*Understanding Prophetic People*, pp. 50, 53).

However, let me give a word of caution here. The contemporary mindset says that if you are truly intelligent, you question everything. Some people will question a prophet just to make themselves look smarter or more spiritually mature. When those questions come from a root of pride or insecurity, the person ends up talking themselves out of a word from God that was meant by the Father to do them good.

The line between the command *test all things* and *believe the prophets and you will prosper,* is very important.

We must be careful not to allow our own preferences, prejudices, and culture to influence any word that we give. Agabus' prophecy to Paul about persecution in Jerusalem in Acts 21 is a good case in point which we covered in Chapter 3. That's why we must obey 1 Corinthians 14:32 which says, *The spirits of the prophets are subject to the prophets.* Such obedience provides a good safeguard for us.

I received a strong word for a lady who needed deliverance from a particular demonic entity. She totally rejected it and tried to say that it was not for her but for her husband. Since she was so adamant, I did not force the issue. Remember, it's the job of the Holy Spirit to convict of sin, not ours. Within a short time, she became seriously ill. Recovery was long, arduous, and painful. During that period of time, as she had to give up abilities, freedoms, and mindsets, the manifestations of that demonic spirit gradually left. She was forced by her illness to stop feeding it. God wants all of us to be free indeed (John 8:36). However, we can choose whether we're willing to receive freedom the easy way by confession, repentance, and turning, or the hard way. Growing a godly character is easier (and faster) if we're willing to rid ourselves of control, preferences, prejudices, and self-will.

Mark it down that you will fail. We won't succeed if we are unwilling to fail in front of people. This is embarrassing. It is especially hard when we've fallen in front of people without grace or mercy. But it will happen and we must learn to deal with it.

But solid food belongs to those who are of full age, that is, those who by reason of use have their senses exercised to discern both good and evil (Hebrews 5:14).

> We won't succeed if we are unwilling to fail.

This is the difference between those who prophesied in the Old Testament and were stoned if the word proved to be false, and we today who are living under the new covenant. When we fail, we will not be stoned for two reasons:

1. We receive our prophecy in a different manner. It comes from within us rather than coming upon us.
2. *For we know in part and we prophesy in part* (1 Corinthians 13:9). *Having then gifts differing according to the grace given to us, let us use them: if prophecy, let us prophesy in proportion to our faith* (Romans 12:6).

Years ago, I was sent a video of a man who claimed to be a prophet. Because of research he'd done, he gave a very strong "prophecy" about a well-known world figure. He also gave a date as to when this man's downfall would happen. He was so certain of his prophecy that he said he'd quit prophesying if his prediction didn't come true. It didn't happen. Because of research I have done on my own about this world figure, I don't doubt that the man will fall. Sometime. But when? The "prophet" didn't stop prophesying, and I don't know if he ever did. But, if he is truly seeking the Lord and wanting to seek the gift of prophesy as we are all commanded to do, I hope he's still trying. Perhaps just not so publicly. Why? Because the nature of learning anything is to fall, get up, fall and get up again and again and again. It's how we all learned to walk; it's how we grow in the Lord.

> *If Jesus had to learn obedience by suffering, we will too!*

When we do fail, we must be willing to admit it rather than cover it up or quit trying.

Mark it down that you will suffer.

Though He was a Son, yet He learned obedience by the things which He suffered (Hebrews 5:8). If Jesus had to learn obedience by suffering, we will too!

Until or unless God releases you, and you have the authority of those to whom you are accountable, limit your prophecy to edification, exhortation, comfort (consolation), worship, and knowing how to pray.

Do not use prophecy to manipulate or control people or circumstances. Again, use the gift with integrity. We must bless, not curse.

Sandford says, "To accurately perceive what is in the heart of another person does not make us prophetic. It makes us human. The more alive we become in our spirits, the more alert and sensitive we become to the hearts of those around us. Wonderful prophetic words, on the other hand, can result as we compassionately identify with the hearts of others, accurately read what is there from the human side, and then turn to seek God for the true word in relation to it" (*Understanding Prophetic People*, pp. 67, 68).

Do not imitate others. Just be yourself and let the gift come out of you according to your own personality. With the pseudo-sophistication of our Western religious intelligentsia, we see the practice of mimicking others taken to an extreme. A person with a gift for teaching or preaching is told he or she must walk around and, at some point in the message, raise their voice and get excited. No. You don't have to put on a show. Just be yourself. If you're comfortable walking around as you speak, walk around. If you're not, don't. Some people prophesy using, "Thus saith the Lord," over and over in their message. Does this make their words more powerful? Or is this a way of covering up insecurity?

When I take someone through deliverance, I talk the same as when I'm having a conversation with them. One time I was working with a woman who already had been through a lot of deliverance from some well-known deliverance ministers. In the middle of our session, she looked at me and began to chuckle. "RaJean," she said. "You are so funny. You just sit quietly in your chair. You don't raise your voice at all. But the demons leave anyway."

It's not because of theatrics that demons flee. It's because of the Name and Blood of Jesus, and the authority of the believer. I know what my authority is over demons; I don't need to yell or scream or grab the person and shake them. Neither does a prophet have to yell and scream to get his or her message across. If that happens because of the emotion behind the message, or God "inspires" him to raise his voice, that's fine. But for a prophet to do so as a means of gaining authority, is unnecessary.

Avoid spiritual weirdness like the plague. God may have you do strange things, but rarely, if ever, will they be bizarre. We are to be naturally supernatural, not unnaturally.

Your gift or intelligence will not make you mature. When we were still in our 20s, Gary encountered a run-away 15-year-old boy. He brought him home, we led him to the Lord and poured the word of God into him. After a time, he was willing to return to his home. Still needing to grow up, he told me that, since he was so intelligent, he was more mature than others his age. But where had his so-called "maturity" gotten him? When Gary found him, he was living with some very wicked people who were taking undue advantage of him in exchange for a place to sleep and a little bit of food. Time, knowledge, experience, trial and error, exposure to others with prophetic giftings, and the work of the fruit of the Spirit in our lives – all of these things working together - will make us mature in the Lord. There is a reason we are told not to put a new believer in positions of leadership (1 Timothy 3:6).

Either make the tree good and its fruit good, or else make the tree bad and its fruit bad; for a tree is known by its fruit (Matthew 12:33).

"Christian maturity denotes a state of being where one is complete in God, thoroughly developed, and fully grown. This maturity reflects being responsible beyond duty, bearing the burdens of others, giving more than you receive, loving more than you are loved, going the extra mile with your brother, endeavoring to keep the unity of the Spirit, and esteeming others better than yourself," says Larry J. Randolph on page 165 of his book, *User Friendly Prophecy*.

"Genuine prophetic ministry releases power and encouragement for building up the people of God to accomplish His will. Mature prophetic people are consumed with concern for others," says Loren Sandford on page 42 of his book, *Understanding Prophetic People*.

"Tools" God uses to speak prophetically

- Visions
- Dreams
- Impressions on your heart without reasoning or inquiry
- Perception – "Spirit awareness" – a sensitivity to the inner nudging of the Holy Spirit.
- Inner voice
- Audible voice
- Mental pictures – what you see in your mind's eye

Today, many are calling for the gift of prophecy to be used in evangelism – to take the gift of the Holy Spirit beyond the four walls of the church. This is a very effective tool to use, but it requires a lot of courage and confidence. God has used me in this way many times and it's always been well received. But it's also scary because of my own pride that I might get it wrong.

GUIDELINES FOR EVALUATING PROPHECIES

The revelation itself. Where did it come from?

The interpretation of the revelation. We must be careful to allow God to give His own definitions to words. If we've received a vision or a dream, we must let Him tell us what things mean. There is no "blanket" meaning for things. God knows not only our personal language but our personal preferences as well. Yet there are literally classes and books written on what objects mean. I believe we need to be very careful with them. Besides, I'd rather hear the Lord give me His interpretation of whatever He shows me.

The application of the interpretation to real life. How and where is it to be given? Publicly, privately, in a small group? Is it to be given in words, in song, dance, or drama? Are you to be forthright in giving it, soft and gentle, with grace, with humor, or with all soberness?

I used to have a friend who often talked about how she needed $5,000 to be able to do what she believed God wanted her to do with her life. I'd speak to her about waiting on the Lord and trusting Him to provide for whatever she needed to fulfill her destiny. But she'd argue that she just needed $5,000. She'd even buy lottery tickets hoping to gain her $5,000 that way. She talked like that for a long time. One day I was in a novelty store and saw they had $1,000 bill play money. (The U.S. Mint no longer prints bills in that denomination.) I bought five of them. Then I made a date to go see my friend. In the course of visiting, I reminded her of her desire for $5,000 which caused her to begin her complaining litany again. When she was through, I calmly said, "Well, you don't have to worry about that anymore," as I handed her the five fake $1,000 bills. She laughed and laughed. Then I gave her the word God had laid on my heart about how she was trusting the lottery instead of trusting Him. She received the word even while appreciating the humor. In fact, she stuck the fake money on her refrigerator as a reminder to change her mindset and trust the Lord.

Many years ago and when I was much thinner, my husband and I were asked to perform a prophetic dance at a women's conference in India. A professional dance instructor provided the choreography so that the prophetic message would be clear to the audience. It was all about what happens when we receive the Lord, are given gifts, and then take pride in our new status as gifted Christians. The dance portrayed how we sometimes claim our giftings as our own, apart from Him, and without staying under His direction and protection. It was incredibly effective, yet not a word was spoken. The prophecy was given strictly through dance. More than a decade later, people who attended that conference were still talking about it whenever they saw us.

Are we even supposed to share what we've received? Remember, you want the receiver to be ready to receive it. If we give a word too soon, it can do more harm than good. One time, I received a word of prophecy for a friend. But I was instructed not to give it to her. I simply used it for prayer and thought that was it. More than eight months later, she asked me if I had a word for her, and I remembered the prophecy. I got it out and gave it to her. She was very receptive and blessed. She asked why I hadn't given it to her when I'd first received it. When I told her God hadn't allowed me to do so, she admitted that she would not have been in a position to have received it, and was glad that I'd waited.

We must take what God gives us and use wisdom in what we do with it. There is, of course, an exception to this rule. God sometimes sends a word of prophecy to someone whom He knows won't receive it. But in His love and grace, He still wants to give them one more chance. Those were the kinds of people to whom God sent Ezekiel to speak. One summer God told me He was going to give me hard words for people to whom He'd send me. I was to take the charge very seriously. He told me that I'd be the last person to speak the Word of Life to them before He would release them to the fullness of their choices.

"Spiritual maturity is not defined by what you know but by what you do with the knowledge you have. Likewise, in regard to prophecy, it is often a greater act of maturity to remain silent than to speak a word out of season," says Larry J. Randolph. (*User Friendly* Prophecy, p. 173)

> *Always make allowances for the immature.*

Always make allowances for the immature. We all have to learn, and, as I've said before, we learn by falling down and getting up. Falling down and getting up. Falling down and getting up.

All prophecy is conditional, in that it is subject not only to conditions placed by God within the text of the prophecy, but by the receptivity of the person it's given to. God made a prophecy to the Israelites in Egyptian bondage that He would bring them into a land of milk and honey. But they were not receptive to receiving it and were not walking in obedience. So, God's word was made null and void – for them. Forty years later, their children became the heirs of the prophetic word that was given to them initially. The opposite was true of Nineveh. They were receptive. The promised judgment didn't fall on them then. It fell 150 years later.

SUMMARY

Any type of spiritual ministry must master the "art" of making God's will simple, understandable, and useable.

Though the word of prophecy coming out of the prophet is important, the basic truth or "word" to be seen is the relationship between the prophet and God. The gift and office of prophecy are not because of what the prophet says, but because of his relationship with God. This relationship is the heart of why I believe Paul urged the Corinthians to seek the gift of prophecy. An intimate, honest relationship with the Father is required before anyone can receive anything from Him for another person.

A clear conscience before all men accompanied by faith is necessary (1 Tim. 1:5).

Therefore, a prophet or prophetess is not important in and of themselves, but because he or she bears a word from the Lord.

The receiver must be careful to hear the word and the One from whom it came, rather than look to the person through whom it came.

The prophet is merely a delegated authority of God to proclaim truth from God to a particular person or group of people.

Becoming a prophetic person and receiving the gift of prophecy is not the same as the office of prophet. I used to believe that for a person to walk in the office of prophet they had to be recognized as such by the local church. And many people, including Loren Sandford, whom I've quoted in this chapter, teach this. But I now know that is not true. A person in the office of an evangelist will evangelize whether or not they have the official sanction of the church. A teacher will examine and look for every little proof whether or not anyone appreciates his diligence. A prophet is a prophet whether or not he or she is recognized as such. And, biblically, they are often not recognized or appreciated. However, "accurate prophetic ministry has the potential to alert us to opportunities before they open up so we can respond quickly and effectively" (R. Loren Sandford, *Understanding Prophetic People*, pp 45-46).

14
DISCERNMENT

The *New World Dictionary of the American Language, Second College Edition* defines the word "discern" as to separate a thing mentally from another or others, to recognize as separate or different. Additionally, it says that discernment is the power of discerning, keen perception or judgment, insight, acumen. That's all it says. There is nothing about the difference between spiritual and carnal discernment, how to get the good kind, or where it comes from.

This chapter is about spiritual discernment.

Besides speaking through the scriptures themselves, the Holy Spirit speaks in dreams, visions, and prophetic words. But much of what is revealed will actually come through our capacity to perceive, to discern correctly, and to know correctly. The scriptures tell us that Jesus "perceived" (which means to know) the thoughts of men *in His Spirit* (Mark 2:8).

Now we have received, not the spirit of the world, but the Spirit who is from God, that we might know the things that have been freely given to us by God. These things we also speak, not in words which man's wisdom teaches but which the Holy Spirit teaches, comparing spiritual things with spiritual. But the natural man does not receive the things of the Spirit of God, for they are foolishness to him; nor can he know them, because they are spiritually discerned. But he who is spiritual judges all things, yet he himself is rightly judged by no one. For who has known the mind of the Lord that he may instruct Him? But we have the mind of Christ (1 Corinthians 2:12-16).

These verses are often used to insist that our view of a person or situation is the only correct one.

- Example: Accusations leveled at people that are not based on fact.
- Example: Peter telling Jesus he would not suffer. Jesus responded by saying, *Get behind Me Satan! You are an offense to Me, for you are not mindful of the things of God but the things of men* (Matthew 16:23).

These are both examples of carnal thinking under the guise of spiritual discernment. Later, I'll share two stories that illustrate these examples. Basically, if we are to move in spiritual discernment, our view of life must be purged of human thoughts and reactions.

To Discern, You Cannot Judge by Your Own Standards

First of all, we need to recognize that the gift of the Holy Spirit talked about in 1 Corinthians 12:10 is the discerning of spirits - not character or motives, or habits, or thoughts, or clothes, or size, or even of actions. Those things are not ours to judge, and we need to stop, for God looks on the heart, not on the external. And that's what we want.

True, godly discernment will not come until we crucify our instinct to judge. We've got to uproot all thought systems that have not been planted in the soil of faith and love for people. This may take a lifetime to do. To appropriate the discernment that is in the *mind of Christ* (1

Corinthians 2:16), we must first find the heart of Christ. The heart and love of Jesus are summed up in His own words: *I did not come to judge the world, but to save the world* (John 12:47).

Spiritual discernment of spirits is the grace to see into the unseen as God sees. It is a gift of the Spirit to perceive what is in the spirit of another person. Its purpose is to see into the nature of that which is veiled. But the first veil that must be removed is the veil over our own hearts. Jesus demands we understand our own need for His mercy so that, out of the grace we have received, we can compassionately minister to others. In this process, of course, we will discover the depravity and selfishness of our own personal, carnal nature. And we will come to know that the gift of discernment is not a faculty of our minds, our own intelligence, or our own spirituality.

We must constantly remind ourselves that Christ's goal is to save, not judge, so that we aren't tempted to judge by external things. We are called to navigate the narrow and well-hidden path into the true nature of human need. Hidden because most Christians want to believe that they have the gift of discernment. Almost every pastor I've ever met truly believes that they have the gift of discernment. I've discovered that very few of them do. I've seen them ignore those who are truly hungry and give attention to those who "play the game" of spirituality.

We knew a certain pastor who professed to have the gift of discernment. Some friends informed us that he was about to invite another man to come into his flock to minister. Fortunately, Gary and I knew from personal experience that the man whom the pastor had invited was a wolf in sheep's clothing. He had a history of dividing friends, marriages, and churches. We were able to convince the pastor not to invite him. However, it took several meetings to do so because the pastor believed he had the gift of discernment.

Unfortunately, against my advice, a female leader of that congregation went to work for the "wolf." She ignored my advice because, after all, she was a "good judge of character." Years later, after experiencing the "fruit" of this wolf, she twice confessed to me that I was absolutely right and she should have listened.

Another pastor made a point of telling me that, as a pastor, he had the gift of discernment. Yet he literally argued with Gary while Gary was giving a testimony about how he used to behave. Gary stopped him by insisting, "No, really, I used to be like that."

A woman, who adamantly claimed to have discernment, once gave me a gift. After opening the gift, admiring it, and thanking her, I absent-mindedly folded the wrapping paper very neatly as we talked. She told me later that she knew I really liked the gift because of how I even "treasured" the wrapping paper. I never told her that was hardly discernment on her part as I had subsequently thrown the used paper away.

If you are to exercise discernment to help people, you must remember that it is a well-hidden path and that you are following a gentle, kind Lamb. These two principles form a foundation that must be laid correctly. Using the gift of discernment means you cannot react. You must make yourself blind to what seems apparent. People may react to you, but . . .

1. You cannot react to them.
2. You must always remain forgiving in nature.

Remember, we're talking about the gift of discerning of spirits, about what is going on inside a person. In the example of Peter and Jesus, Peter clearly demonstrated carnal discernment while Jesus showed true spiritual discernment as He addressed the spirit that was using Peter's mouth. You too may be dealing with demons who speak to you in a person's voice, masquerading as the individual. You may also be hearing unhealed hurt and pain. That's why we need the gift of discerning of spirits. For this very reason, Jesus said, *Anyone who speaks a word against the Son of Man, it will be forgiven him* (Matthew 12:32). Jesus was prepared in His heart to forgive us before we ever sinned against Him. He knew His mission was to die for men, not condemn them.

We are not only called into Christ's life but into His mission as well. Jesus said, *As You sent Me into the world, I also have sent them into the world* (John 17:18).

We are called to die, that others may live. Therefore, we must realize that before our perception develops, before we have true discernment, our love must develop until our normal attitude is one of forgiveness. A characteristic of the orphan spirit is the lack of basic trust. Basic trust is when you risk being vulnerable with an open heart even when it hurts you to stay open and not close your spirit. It is when you are able to move beyond weaknesses in others, receive God's healing touch, and not run away.

If God will show us the hearts of men and use us to release them from captivity, we cannot react to what they say. As our perception becomes more like that of Christ Himself and men's hearts are revealed to us, we cannot react to what they think or say.

If we do not move in divine forgiveness, we will walk in much deception. We will presume we have discernment when, in truth, we are seeing through the lens of a critical spirit. We must know our weaknesses, for if we are blind to our sins, what we assume we discern in others will merely be a reflection of ourselves.

A friend of mine got very upset when her new sister-in-law, who was hosting the family Thanksgiving dinner, asked her to bring a salad. "A salad!" my friend stormed. "I'm the best cook in the family and she asked me to bring a salad that anyone can throw together?" She perceived that this new relative was discounting her by asking her to bring a simple salad. Fortunately, she went on a rant about this request over the phone with me before calling her new sister-in-law. As soon as I got a chance, I said, "Well now let's look at this more closely. She is new to the family and all of your family members are very strong people. It sounds to me like she is insecure and very nervous. She is simply trying to make sure that the meal will be well received so that she'll get the approval of the family." My friend considered the possibility and calmed down. When she finally called the sister-in-law, before expressing her outrage, she queried the gal about how she was handling the hosting of the entire extended family. The poor girl was so nervous about it, she was literally going to take two days off work just to prepare. And later, she learned that the girl was totally intimidated by my friend. As the oldest and the only girl in a family of boys, my friend had helped her mother raise the boys and had done much of the cooking. Consequently, when the boys later married, they not only raved about her meals, they compared their wives' cooking with hers. No wonder this new sister-in-law was nervous! My friend immediately repented of her carnal discernment and was very thankful that she had been given another perspective. If we do not move in love, we will actually become a menace to others.

This is exactly what Jesus taught when He said, *Judge not, that you be not judged. For with what judgment you judge, you will be judged; and with the measure you use, it will be measured back to you. And why do you look at the speck in your brother's eye, but do not consider the plank in your own eye? Or how can you say to your brother, 'Let me remove the speck from your eye'; and look, a plank is in your own eyes? Hypocrite! First remove the plank from your own eye, and then you will see clearly to remove the speck from your brother's eye* (Matthew 7:1-5).

Repentance is the removal of the "planks" in our eyes; it brings about the ability to see clearly and with kindness. There are many who believe they have the Lord's discernment concerning something or someone. Perhaps in some things they do. But many are simply judging others carnally and calling it discernment. Psychology is helpful but is not discernment. It's studied deductive reasoning. Some have studied body language and they judge based on that knowledge and call it discernment. This is not the gift of discernment. It is a judgment based on study and what the eye sees. It is making judgments based on the external, not the discerning of spirits. Jesus commanded us to judge not. That's why I said in the beginning that we have no business making judgments about people based on their clothes or size or words or actions.

I don't know who made this statement, but it fits perfectly here, "The same Eternal Hand that wrote the Law on stones in the Old Covenant is writing the Law of the Kingdom on tablets of flesh today. This word to 'judge not' is just as immutably final as His Ten Commandments. It is still God speaking."

The Goal Is to See Clearly

The judgmental carnal mind always sees the image of itself in others. Without realizing that it is seeing a reflection of itself, it assumes it perceives others with true discernment. Jesus said that the person who judges is a hypocrite. The Lord is not saying we should stop observing other people and being aware of their needs. He wants us to be able to help one another. The emphasis in Jesus' command to *judge not* is summarized in His concluding remark: *First remove the plank from your own eye and then you will see clearly to remove the speck from your brother's eye* (Matthew 7:5).

The way we help is not by judging, but by seeing clearly! The last thing we want to hear Jesus say to us is what He said to Peter: *You are an offense to Me* (Matthew 16:23). And we do not see clearly until we have been through deep and thorough repentance – until the instinct to judge after the flesh is uprooted! When we see clearly, it will always be with compassion, understanding, and forgiveness.

Example 1: I had a friend whose husband divorced her after years of his unfaithfulness. Because there was a divorce support group in our church at the time, she decided to join it. After a few meetings, however, she left the group. Why? Was it because she didn't want to deal with the pain and look at her stuff? No. It was because she was getting judgment from the leader and other members of the group. She wasn't going through the stages of grief along with them. They did not take into consideration the fact that her husband had multiple affairs during the course of their 35-year marriage. Neither had he ever been supportive of her, and had left her two years before he filed divorce papers. She'd already worked through most, if not all, of those stages. What she needed was encouragement in trying to figure out how to support herself and their mentally-challenged, adult son. She'd joined the group because she thought they'd provide that support. But unfortunately, all she got was judgment which was not based on fact.

Example 2: I received a long email from a young mother whom I'd been mentoring. It contained one accusation after another for things I didn't even say or do. Judgment, judgment, judgment. I was very hurt by her accusations, so I went to God to receive His view of the situation, and get His love for her. God not only healed my hurt and gave me love for her, but He also assured me that I was not guilty. Then He gave me true discernment about her. The accusations were not based on things I'd done or said, but on what her mother had said and done. The young mother had just gone through a miscarriage of a baby that she and her husband had wanted very much. Her mother, whom she didn't get along with, came to "help" her recuperate and care for her two-year-old. It didn't take long for her mother to voice her difference of opinion regarding child-rearing. She told her daughter what she was doing wrong and even went so far as to call her a bad mother. And that's what she accused me of telling her. Attacking someone when they are in grief and very vulnerable is not fair. In fact, it is mean-spirited. For this reason, I'd made a point of building this young mother up during our mentoring sessions because God had shown me that she was very insecure. After reading and praying over her email, the discernment the Lord gave me was that her rant against me was what she wanted to say to her mother but didn't. I was safe. Her mother wasn't. This is a good example of a judgment by accusation that was not based on fact. Many of our judgments of each other in the Body of Christ are just like that. We project on another person what someone else did or said, and call it discernment. On the other hand, true discernment can not only bring healing but enable us to help the other person.

We also sometimes have "discernment" about another that is based on what the Holy Spirit is really saying to us about ourselves that we don't want to accept.

Example 3: A woman we knew, whom I'll call Sally, often dressed and acted in a masculine way. One day while praying in church, Sally received a "word" from God for "Jane" who was sitting beside her. The word was that Jane needed to get more in touch with her feminine side. Jane was shocked at the word but, wanting to receive whatever God had for her, went home and told her husband so they could pray about it. She wanted to make any necessary changes. Her husband said he didn't need to pray because he'd never known anyone who was more feminine than Jane. What Sally did is called transference. She transferred what God was telling her to Jane. There may also have been a bit of jealousy involved too. Jealousy can be a big "plank" in a person's eye. Jealousy is often rooted in low self-esteem and is accompanied by judgment disguised as discernment.

Example 4: When I was a young mother, another young mother accused me of not sharing my own personal struggles with her and others, which was true. Her concluding "discernment" as to why I didn't was because I was self-righteous. The truth of the matter was that I was going through one of the hardest struggles of my life at the time and I truly wanted to share my pain with someone else. But I'd learned the hard way in the past to choose carefully those with whom I shared personal information. I'd put out some feelers, which I knew anyone who was truly discerning and wanted to come alongside me to help, would pick up on. Some of those feelers I'd intentionally directed toward her since she held a position of authority in the church. But there was a "plank" in her eye and she couldn't see me clearly. Her "discernment" was a false judgment.

From these four examples and the Matthew 7 scripture, we can see that Jesus paralleled speaking to people about their sins, with taking specks out of their own eyes. The eye is perhaps the most tender and sensitive part of the human body. How do you take a speck out of someone's eye? Very carefully! You must first win their trust. This entails consistently demonstrating an attitude that does not judge or instinctively condemn. Beyond that, it involves knowing and acknowledging the facts and getting any "planks" out of your own eyes. Then, if what you have to say to someone is important, you ask for their undivided attention. That's the way God usually deals with us. He usually doesn't speak to us until we slow down, tune out the static of our world, and give Him our attention. To walk in true discernment, our hearts must be quiet before God, and we must learn how to listen.

To summarize:

1. We must see clearly to help others by dealing with our own "stuff."
2. We must be able to see where a person's vision is obstructed.
3. We must develop trust in our relationship with them.
4. Only then, remove their "speck" without judging or condemning them.

If you seek to have a heart that does not condemn, and you crucify your instinct to judge, you will have laid a true foundation for the gift of discernment of spirits. Your heart will also be prepared to receive dreams, visions, and insights from God. You will be unstained by human bias and corruption.

15

APOSTOLIC PRAYER

During the days of the Roman Empire, every Italian ship had an apostle on board. His job was to make sure everyone else had what they needed to do their job and knew how to do it. It was his responsibility to make sure the work on the ship ran smoothly and efficiently. The Greek meaning of apostle is an ambassador or commissioner. In scripture, it is an office in the church.

And He Himself gave some to be apostles, some prophets, some evangelists, and some pastors and teachers, for the equipping of the saints for the work of ministry, for the edifying of the body of Christ, till we all come to the unity of the faith and of the knowledge of the Son of God, to a perfect man, to the measure of the stature of the fullness of Christ (Ephesians 4:11-13).

This list of offices is more about function than it is hierarchy. There is no up or down in importance or rank. If God is anything, He is consistent, and there is to be no hierarchy in the church of God. How do we know this? There are two proofs:

1. In context, this list is all about what the people holding these offices are to do - equip and edify the saints. It's not about their title or how important they are. There are many people

today claiming the title of Apostle who are not equipping the saints for the work of ministry. There are even more pastors who aren't equipping the saints. Instead, they try to do all the work and have trouble delegating.

2. The Apostle Paul did not regard James, who was the head of the church in Jerusalem, as anything more than a fellow believer, living out his particular calling. When Paul and Barnabus had a dispute in Antioch with some Pharisees over Gentiles being circumcised, the church there sent them to the church in Jerusalem to get a corporate decision on the matter from *the church, the apostles and elders.* Note the order of the listing in Acts 15:4. The church as a whole is first, then apostles and elders. Both Peter and James gave their opinion but it was the apostles, elders, and the whole church that made the decision about the matter (Acts 15:22-29). Years later, in telling the Galatians about the dispute, Paul said they went there to consult with *those who seemed to be something, whatever they were, it makes no difference to me; God shows personal favoritism to no man - for those who seemed to be something added nothing to me* (Galatians 2:6).

A third proof, which I won't go into detail about here, is that when talking about the offices and functions within the Body of Christ, it is all about honor. Honoring one another and each other's gifts

> *It is all about honor.*

and calling is an absolute requirement in biblical Christianity. In fact, Paul taught that because of the dishonoring of one another in the Body, many are sick and even die (I Corinthians 11:25-30).

Let us consider one another in order to stir up love and good works, not forsaking the assembling of ourselves together, as is the manner of some, but exhorting one another, and so much the more as you see the Day approaching (Hebrews 10:24-25).

We need to look at that word, "assembling." It does not mean gathering together. For instance, if you purchase a large boxed item at the store, the box often will be marked "some assembly required." Later, when you get home and open the box, you discover that not everything inside is completely assembled. You have some work to do putting it together. And if you lose a piece or just don't bother using all the pieces that were in the box, it's not properly assembled. You must honor the manufacturer who knew just what pieces were required for the item to work properly. You must recognize the importance and honor the work of each piece, no matter how seemingly insignificant it is. For the item to be effective and function as it was designed by its manufacturer, every piece must be in its proper place – every piece must be acknowledged and honored as critical to the item's successful assembly and intended use.

That's how it is with the body of Christ. We must honor God by honoring each member of the body and the part they have been given for the entire body to fulfill its God-given purpose. This is so important that Paul said we must not forsake assembling - honoring and using - ourselves together. And this is in the context of stirring up love and good works.

Paul further emphasized this honoring of one another in his comparison of the members of the church to the parts of our physical bodies (1 Corinthians 12:12-31).

How does this relate to the topic of apostolic prayer? Knowing what an apostle is and isn't, the duties and function, gives us direction if we are to pray and minister apostolically, i.e., like an apostle.

Let's take the definition of apostle as an ambassador. The apostle Paul said, *we are ambassadors for Christ* (2 Corinthians 5:20). This statement is in the context of him saying, *if anyone is in Christ, he is a new creation* (Verse 17).

Yes, he's talking specifically about himself and those who traveled with him. But in the broader context of the passage, he's explaining who a born-again believer is. What is an ambassador? Generally speaking, an ambassador is someone who is a citizen of one country who represents that country in another country where he doesn't have citizenship. That's us! Our citizenship is in heaven. We are simply heaven's ambassadors here on earth. An ambassador is under authority, accountable to others. Again, that's us! You and me! This is probably why many people define apostle as one who is sent. And that, too, is us. We may not hold the office of apostle, but we're to do everything apostolically, as one who is sent.

If we take the definition of apostle as a commissioner, that fits us too. Paul and Barnabus were commissioned and sent out by the church in Antioch (Acts 13:1-3). They, in turn, commissioned elders in the churches they established. That's what those in the office of apostle are to do. But if we are fulfilling our job as God's representatives here on earth, we too will do our part in bringing people to Christ, making sure they are discipled, and encouraging them to fulfill their particular calling. It's called ministering apostolically.

With this in mind, exactly what is Apostolic Prayer? It is exactly that - praying apostolically. Being under the authority of God and the Holy Scriptures. Praying with accountability. Coming into agreement with others, just as Paul did over the matter of circumcision.

ACCOUNTABILITY

We are accountable to God. And He has given us the guideline for how that works.

Now this is the confidence that we have in Him, that if we ask anything according to His will, He hears us. And if we know that He hears us, whatever we ask, we know that we have the petitions that we have asked of Him (1 John 5:14-15).

INFORMED PRAYER

We are accountable to God by following His will, His word, and His way. What's His will? Apostolic prayer is informed prayer. An apostolic intercessor will continually be a student of God's word. When I first learned about this, because I have trouble remembering the address of a passage, I began to write in the back of my Bible every time I found a scripture that tells how to pray for something. If we want our prayers answered, and if we're going to be under authority, we need to know how to pray and then follow the instructions of scripture. So, look it up!

My husband and I were invited to speak to a group one day and field questions. When input from the group was allowed, some began to talk about deliverance. From the flow of the discussion, I could tell that, much to my surprise, some of them had inaccurate teaching as to what to do with demons. So, ever the teacher, I acknowledged that we don't actually have any specific direction in scripture as to where to tell demons to go. Therefore, I always just tell them to go to the feet of Jesus and go wherever He tells them to go. But, I included, we are not told to send them to dry places. Why? Because they don't like the dry places and will gather other demons and return to the one from whom they were cast out (Matthew 12:43-45, Luke 11:24-26). After the meeting, one lady belligerently told Gary, "I don't accept what RaJean said. Jesus told me to send them to dry places so that is what I will continue to do!" When Gary later relayed what she said to me, I responded, "Well, it wasn't Jesus who told her that!" She was not only unteachable but in rebellion.

At the time of this writing, an unscriptural practice has become very prevalent here in the United States that concerns prayer. Jesus clearly said, *Whatever you ask the Father in My name, He will give it to you* (John 16:23). He reiterated this command when He went on to say, *Until now you have asked nothing in My name. Ask, and you will receive, that your joy may be full* (verse 24). Then He repeated Himself in verses 26-27.

In spite of this very clear instruction by the Master Himself, many people begin their prayers by saying, *Our Father in heaven.* Then they conclude their prayers with, "In Your name, we pray, amen." Yet, we've never been told to pray in the name of the Father. And, the name of Jesus is never mentioned anywhere in their prayer.

I've pondered this and questioned God as to why they would do this. The only answers I've come up with are that they are either ignorant of what Jesus said, they are rebellious, they are ashamed to say the name of Jesus in public, or they just don't care if their prayer is answered or not.

If we need to be accountable to God, we must be informed as to how to pray and how to go about spiritual warfare. Even King David, the man known to be *a man after God's own heart* (1 Samuel 13:14, Acts 13:22). was willing to allow the Lord to *train his hands for war* (2 Samuel 22:35, Psalm 144:1). Can we do less?

In being accountable to God, we also need to recognize our own boundaries, our gifts and calling, and what our sphere of authority is that God has sovereignly given us. What's your authority? For example, Gary and I can pray anywhere in the United States because we're citizens. This is our country. We have authority here. We can pray with even more authority in Texas than we can in Colorado because we're residents of Texas. We have still more authority to pray in and over the 24-county East Gate region of Texas because we not only live in the region, but we hold accountability within a state-wide ministry for this part of Texas. But we've learned to take this matter of authority and accountability even further. When we go to minister in a specific locale, we try to identify an effective ministry that we can be accountable to in that area. We do not want to bring division in the Body of Christ. Neither do we want to go into an area as "experts" who know more than the people who live there. We want to build up, encourage, and unify God's people. I have authority to pray for the nation when I go to DC because that city belongs to all US citizens. But I always choose to come under the authority of ministries that headquarter there. When we go to another country, we do the same thing. We seek accountability. That's what the apostles on those Roman ships did. As soon as they docked at a foreign port, they checked in under that country's port authorities. We should too.

Being informed is also about knowing the facts on the ground. What is the history of the person, place, or situation we're praying about? We don't have to know everything but, at the same time, we don't want to be presumptuous either. Apostolic intercessors are researchers, interested in history. I've known intercessors who go into prayer for a person or territory with the assumption that the Holy Spirit will show them what to pray. He does an excellent job of doing that by giving us Words of Wisdom and Words of Knowledge. However, we have sometimes missed the mark because we were too lazy to do the nitty-gritty work of research. When God gives me a prayer assignment, I've often done a lot of research, primarily because without the research, I don't know what questions I should ask of Him. I've had a lot of people want to go with me on prayer assignments, but only if I don't ask them to help with the research. I understand that because, unless you're a real history buff, digging into history can be a hard, arduous task. But the benefits are incredible when you take what you've learned, offer it up to Him, and see what He tells you to do about it. A priority of being an apostolic intercessor is having a teachable spirit and the willingness to get your hands dirty and do the work.

The apostle on a Roman ship had to learn a lot of things before he was given the responsibility for a ship. He had to learn how a ship worked, and what kind of skills were needed by the people he hired to run the ship. He also had to know how to navigate, and how to find the ocean currents which the Bible calls paths of the sea (Psalm 8:8).

> *Apostolic prayer is about being informed.*

Do you get the picture? First, apostolic prayer is about being informed by lining up with the Word of God, lining up with our fellow believers, and lining up with what's gone before.

There has been much damage caused in the Body of Christ over the teaching of "covering." I don't like that word because it is too broad and is often misused. Biblically the only time the word covering is used is like a blanket or box that gives protection to the object or person being covered. It is never used that way in the New Testament. As we've already seen from scripture, it is accountability that we should seek.

For example, when we started Vawtermark Ministries as a 501(c)3, we asked five pastors of different denominations to allow us to be accountable to them. They all said yes. But one of them took our request as a mere covering, due to the office he held in his denomination, and because we were members of his congregation. Yet he didn't want to receive our newsletters or to know what we were doing. How could he give us advice or correction if he didn't know what we were doing? He believed his job title was a covering. That had nothing to do with his responsibility to be someone to whom we could be accountable. This has happened to us more than once. And we have seen it occur in the lives of others. The result is that the American church has a lot of people trying to function in the fullness of what God has given and equipped them to do, but they are not really accountable to anyone. They have no one who is looking out for them. This is a dangerous situation. Somehow, people don't seem to understand that Jeremiah 17:9 actually applies to them.

The heart is deceitful above all things, and desperately wicked; Who can know it? (Jeremiah 17:9).

To find a listing of apostolic prayer requirements, let's look at what the apostle Paul had to say in Ephesians chapter 1.

Before telling the Ephesians what he was praying for them, we can see that his heart was pure towards them. He'd paid attention to what had been going on with them, particularly their faith level. He was informed. He prayed for them without ceasing. At that time in the Greek world, *without ceasing* was often used to describe a hacking cough. Apostolic prayer is like that - consistent. Always there. Prayer without ceasing is actually a lifestyle.

Here's what Paul prayed in Ephesians 1:

- Verse 16 - He prayed prayers of thanksgiving for them. (This is always a good start since we're supposed to thank God *for* everything (Ephesians 5:20) as well as *in* everything (1 Thessalonians 5:18 and Philippians 4:6).
- Verse 17 - He prayed for a spirit of wisdom.
- Verse 17 - He prayed for a spirit of revelation in the knowledge of God, that they would know God in an ever-deepening intimacy.
- Verse 18 - He prayed that the eyes of their heart and understanding would be enlightened.
- Verse 18 - He prayed that they would know what was the hope of God's calling, His plan for their lives.
- Verse 18 - He prayed that they would know about the riches of the glory of God's inheritance in the saints.
- Verse 19 - He prayed that they would know how much power/ energy/ability God is willing to extend to those who believe.

Wow! That's what we want to pray for ourselves and for everybody we know. That's a true apostolic prayer. Out of the box. Impossible. But God is the God of the impossible.

Summary

Apostolic prayer has to do with:

- Praying as an ambassador
- Praying as a commissioner
- Praying with honor toward the person, place, or situation
- Praying while being accountable to God, scripture, and others
- Praying with an informed understanding of scripture, God's will and way, and understanding of the situation
- Praying with humility
- Praying without ceasing.

16

DISCIPLINED INTERCESSION FOR GROUPS

Many people are glass-half-full people. Generally optimistic and cheerful, they are often satisfied with "good enough." On the other hand, glass-half-empty people are considered pessimistic and critical. True prophets are often accused of this - of only seeing the glass-half-empty, nit-picky, and too particular. That's because they are concerned with obeying all of the details of God's instructions. Look at the following biblical examples:

- King Saul had a "good enough" mindset. In fact, he was happy when Samuel came to him after winning a great battle. With great boasting, he told the prophet, *Blessed are you of the Lord! I have performed the commandment of the Lord* (1 Samuel 15:13). But Samuel was not so happy. In fact, he was so grieved that he reprimanded Saul and pronounced a severe judgment on him - one that Saul fought against for the rest of his life. In true prophet fashion, Samuel made his now-famous statement, *To obey is better than sacrifice, and to heed than the fat of rams* (1 Samuel 15:22). As if that weren't harsh enough, Samuel went on to point out the root of Saul's "good enough" attitude which is rebellion. He explained, *For rebellion is as the sin of witchcraft, and stubbornness is as iniquity and idolatry* (vs. 23). Whoa! That would be hard to hear, wouldn't it?

- After a succession of wicked kings, Hezekiah came to the throne of Judah (2 Chronicles 29-32). *He did what was right in the sight of the Lord* (29:2). Because he followed his heart with action, he was able to turn the nation around, drawing the people into the prescribed worship of the Lord. God blessed to the extent that *he was exalted in the sight of all nations thereafter* (32:23). Unfortunately, he became sick and was near death. Fortunately, *he prayed to the Lord; and He spoke to him and gave him a sign* (vs. 24). Unfortunately (again), *Hezekiah did not repay according to the favor shown him, for his heart was lifted up; therefore wrath was looming over him and over Judah and Jerusalem* (vs. 25). Fortunately, the King repented, but the damage had been done and the glass was still half empty because of his period of pride. The Lord's prophetic pronouncement was that the wrath of God wouldn't come upon the people as long as Hezekiah lived, but would take place afterward (vs. 26). Whew! Hezekiah escaped. But to a culture that was very mindful of the generations, this was just as harsh a consequence as that given to King Saul.

Sometimes things are "good enough" and even prophets have to learn to live with "it" - whatever "it" is. But God often tells us to do something that becomes a matter of simple, detailed obedience. The previous two stories are good examples of how and why God requires the true prophets to be so "nit-picky." They are not an excuse for those who claim prophetic giftings to go around criticizing people. We must note that the prophet Samuel was so grieved about King Saul's actions that he spent an entire night crying out in intercession for the King (1 Samuel 15:11). This kind of response can be seen in every case where a prophet of God is required to reprimand someone. It comes from a heart of love and fear of the Lord. Even then, each prophet had to wait for the Lord to tell him *if* he was to speak to the matter, *how* he was to speak if the answer was yes, and *when* he was to do so.

As prayer and intercession have increased across the world, many who pray are being called by their church, ministry leaders, or directly by the Lord to lead prayer groups. Willing to serve, these new prayer leaders are often ignorant as to how to help their group grow deeper and more effective in the work of prayer. Therefore, God has pressed me to share with you some of what I have learned so far. Some of what I've included in this chapter has already been mentioned in other chapters. But it is worth repeating again because any prayer warrior is disciplined. I expect various responses ranging from, "preach on, sister!" to "you're just being critical." I'm okay with either, because, truthfully, your response is between you and God.

1. The first thing that must happen, for a prayer group to grow in its effectiveness, is a willingness to discipline themselves so they can move from prayer into intercession. "What's the difference?" you may ask. Prayer is talking to God, praying scriptures you are familiar with, and lifting up needs based on what you know. Intercession happens when we lay all that aside, worship Him and wait on the Lord to show us what He wants us to pray. The prayers come directly from the Spirit of God and agree with what Jesus is praying (Romans 8:27, 34). He may give us scriptures, prayers, prophecies, visions, or even prophetic acts to perform. But it all comes from Him, not our flesh or knowledge. Following is an example that happened when Gary and I were a part of such a prayer group. After the group spent time waiting on the Lord, we were led to pray for people in the area around the Black Sea. Sound strange? It did to us too. Nevertheless, the group obeyed by following God's guidance as to how to pray. No one grasped at straws to figure out what to pray, we just waited for the Lord to give us direction. Right before our meeting the next week, we learned that U.S. troops were being moved into the area bordering the Black Sea in Turkey. God had used us as their forward guard.

When teaching in another country on the subject of how to hear the voice of God, I asked for a time of silence so all could hear whatever the Lord might want to speak to them. Instead of silence, the group of 600 women began to pray out loud as was their custom. When repeated pleas for silence went unheeded, I resorted to a term that my mother taught me was never proper. At the top of my lungs, I yelled, "shut up!" I was horrified at what I'd done. But the room immediately got quiet. The Holy Spirit fell, and prophetic words began to arise out of the group of women as they heard God speak to them directly. They learned an important lesson that day that applies to all of us. It is a lot easier to hear God speak when we aren't speaking ourselves.

Most Christian pastors and leaders are not comfortable with silence during a service. One or two minutes is all they will allow. Most congregations are the same way. The more mature a group is, however, the longer they are able to tolerate silence. The prayer group we were a part of at that time was made up of mature, experienced intercessors. I remember on one occasion, we worshipped the Lord, then waited for direction which was our custom. We waited in absolute silence. And we waited. And waited. We didn't want to move in the flesh, so we continued to wait on God – for over an hour and a half. It was then that the Lord prophetically told us that because we had refused to be uncomfortable in the silence, but took comfort in His Presence with obedience, we'd thwarted a major attack the enemy had planned against our city. Wow! We were all amazed. Surely, the ways of the Lord are not our ways.

2. The second principle to follow is absolutely necessary. For a group to advance, each member of the group, especially the leader, must spend time with the Lord in repentance before the meeting. This is part of what the Old Testament priests and Levites did as they consecrated themselves to the service of the Lord in the Temple. The reason I say it's necessary to take care of this in advance is that when anyone comes into the Presence of the Lord or the Spirit falls on

the group during worship, we are immediately aware of His holiness and our uncleanness. Our natural inclination is to start repenting of everything that comes to mind. This is good and is of the Lord. Intercessors, who desire to enter into the service of the King in a group setting, must first allow Him to show them what they need to confess and repent of before the meeting when they are alone. Then, when the Spirit invades the group, each member will be able to immediately "press in" beyond themselves into more of Him. On occasion, even the most mature intercessor will be convicted of something in a group setting. In such a case, that person should confess and repent quietly to the Lord, within themselves, without disturbing what the Holy Spirit wants to do with the group.

The first time I heard the term, "press in," was by a well-known leader. I didn't understand what he meant. He'd started the meeting with worship. At the height of the worship, I didn't understand why he didn't start to lead us in prayer. Instead, he just kept saying, "Press in." Only later did I realize that prayer and intercession are actually about us, and life here on earth, which takes the focus off of the Lord and onto things concerning the earthly realm. He was wanting us to press into the Lord and go higher. It is, after all, from the higher realm, as we are *"seated with Him in the heavenlies"* (Ephesians 2:6) that we can hear His voice more clearly.

This point is critical because failure to observe this discipline will short-circuit the efforts of the entire group. Leaders who do not prepare before the prayer meeting are often prone to confess sin (often using general terms such as "we") and prevent the group from pressing in. I've been in prayer groups where the leader constantly used the group prayer time to confess personal sins. Sometimes, they would generalize under the false assumption that everyone else had the same besetting sins, thus projecting those sins onto others. If leaders are not able to discipline themselves in prayer, they will not only stifle the group but will not be able to stop a group member from doing the same thing.

3. <u>The third point has to do with keeping the group focused</u>. When we pray in the privacy of our own homes, it is not unusual for our minds, and prayers, to move quickly from one topic to another. That's alright unless the Lord tells us differently of course. But if a prayer group does this, it will cause the prayer time to fall short of what God wants to accomplish. Leaders must be very sensitive to this, which I call "tossed salad prayers." (A piece of lettuce here, then a tomato, an onion, some carrot, and some more lettuce, all mixed together.) Unfortunately, many leaders engage in this type of prayer themselves so they don't stop a group member from doing so. However, the leader's job is to help the group focus. Whenever the Body of Christ is together, we need to take advantage of all the giftings God has placed in our members (1 Corinthians 14:26). When a need is presented, time should be given for others to speak out and pray according to the leading of the Lord on the same matter. Experienced prayer leaders have been known to interrupt someone who begins tossed salad praying by saying, "Wait a minute, does anyone else have a prayer on the current topic?" Surprisingly, this never interrupts the flow of the Spirit. Instead, it facilitates what He wants to accomplish through the group. When no one has anything else to pray on that subject, they can move on to another topic which is often what the "tossed salad" person was going to pray next.

4. <u>Part of the prayer leader's responsibility is to encourage participation by each member of the group</u>. At the conclusion of a prayer time, someone invariably approaches the leader saying, "When we were praying about "xyz," I had a vision (or an insight or a scripture). I have concluded that either ignorance, pride, fear, or an unholy view of themselves is the reason such people don't share what God gives them at the appropriate time. I say ignorance because such a person does not truly recognize the truth of 1 Corinthians 12:7. *The manifestation of the Spirit is given to each one for the profit of all.* I say pride because they want the kind of recognition that would

come if the leader were to specifically ask them for input. Fear can be because of being wrong, of not speaking correctly, or because of a past bad experience. This kind of fear requires inner healing to overcome. Finally, when we don't accept the view that God has toward us, it is disbelief that God means what He says about our own personal worth. These things must be corrected for the proper working of any group.

When a prayer leader has a person share in such a way after the meeting is concluded, it is their job, as the group's leader, to seek those people out and find out why. If there are members of the group who never pray, the leader needs to follow up with them also. To follow scripture, every leadership position is given by God for the purpose of teaching, mentoring, mothering, and fathering others (Ephesians 4:12). *We should no longer be children* (vs. 14). Both leader and follower must *grow up* (vs. 15). That's because the Lord's goal is that the whole Body of Christ be *joined and knit together by what every joint supplies, according to the effective working by which every part does its share, causes growth of the body for the edifying of itself in love* (vs. 16).

When these four principles for group prayer are followed by both leaders and members, amazing times of intercession invariably happen and the Kingdom of God is advanced. In giving these principles am I picking on leaders? Yes! Even our secular world knows that leaders are responsible for the people under their authority. Every leadership position incorporates the need to teach the followers whatever is necessary for the job. Whether leaders fulfill their duty through the gift of teacher, exhortation, mercy, giver, etc., they *receive a stricter judgment* (James 3:1). We are accountable to God as to how we fulfill our assignment. That's why we need the whole Body of Christ with each member functioning properly. After listing a litany of how we each sin and fall short of perfection, James gives us information on why we need to be careful as leaders. He also presents the antidote – the key: *Submit to God. Resist the devil and he will flee from you. Draw near to God and*

He will draw near to you. Cleanse your hands, you sinners, and purify your hearts, you double-minded. Lament and mourn and weep! Let your laughter be turned to mourning and your joy to gloom. Humble yourselves in the sight of the Lord, and He will lift you up (James 4:7-10). Be sure to pay attention to the order in which each action is listed. It's important.

We can do this because all things of God begin with Him, with prayer, and back to Him again. Let's get it right, following the guidelines given in scripture, and through the experience of other saints.

17

WARFARE RUTS

Have you noticed that we tend to be creatures of habit? We each have a routine we follow before going to bed or getting up in the morning. We tend to drive to work the same way every day instead of exploring side roads. A woman I know always turns to her right after entering a store to shop. How we approach life often falls into such patterns. Such routine personal habits are sometimes described as ruts. These ruts can be funny, annoying, harmful, or inconsequential. The questions we need to ask ourselves are: Do we do the same thing with God? Is our spiritual life in a rut? What about our approach to spiritual warfare?

For far too many of us, the answers to these questions are obvious. Since we are prone to prefer the familiar, how can we identify our personal "ruts?" It often takes someone else to point them out to us. Such ruts tend to be incorporated into the doctrine or practice of groups of people so I'm going to give you some examples.

When I first learned about the necessity of spending time with God every day, I was a young mother. I asked around for advice. Someone told me that my quiet time should be first thing in the morning. Since I was usually awakened early by a baby crying, and demanding attention, that didn't work for me. Someone else told me that each day should begin with having my devotions the night before. I tried that. Alas! With three babies, two still in diapers, I ended up falling asleep in exhaustion each evening. Finally, I did what has since become a life habit. I asked the Lord to show me what would work for my situation. He showed me a verse that basically said, "I am the God of the arising." That was a personal Rhema word that fit my situation. I knew God was telling me He understood so He would wake me when He wanted me to spend time with Him. That has not always been the case, as my life situation has changed many times through the years. But it worked for me then and set my mind at ease. In fact, it caused me to go to bed each night with excitement and expectation of God waking me up in the middle of the night. That was also the beginning of a lifetime of enough flexibility to be called to the night watch of prayer. What works for me might not work for you and vice versa. God has made us each unique and with different giftings and callings.

Since the topic of this chapter is "Warfare Ruts," let's look at that specifically to identify some ruts we may have fallen into. We all need to be trained for spiritual warfare just as David was trained for secular warfare (Psalm 144:1, 2 Samuel 22:35). Military men and women are trained using set methods with the goal of learning basic skills so they can be flexible enough to handle any situation that might come up. Such skill and flexibility are what enabled American forefathers to win the American Revolutionary War. British forces were used to what had been standard warfare in which the soldiers lined up shoulder-to-shoulder and marched in rows straight toward the opposing army who were lined up the same way. They didn't know what to do when the colonists didn't fight the same way. The colonists often set traps, shot from all directions, engaged in surprise attacks, appeared out of seemingly nowhere, and disguised themselves so they weren't easy targets. Yet when it comes to spiritual warfare in today's climate, many are engaging (and teaching) spiritual warfare much like the British taught secular warfare. Sometimes God may want us to do a sneak attack or engage in a different strategy than we've done before. Here are some examples of spiritual warfare "rules" being taught and practiced that have become ruts.

"Wait for the sound of marching in the Mulberry trees"

This is often quoted from I Chronicles 14:15. But contrast this example with Luke 17:6 – *So the Lord said, "If you have faith as a mustard seed, you can say to this mulberry tree, be pulled up by the roots and be planted in the sea,' and it would obey you."* I'm aware that some translations don't use the word, "mulberry." But that doesn't change the point that God might have something different in mind. Sometimes we may need to wait for a particular sign from God to happen like a sound coming from the trees; other times we may need to just get in there and pull some trees up!

"Judah goes first"

This teaching usually refers to the idea that spiritual warfare should be led by all that Judah stood for. It is taken from Numbers 2:9 - *All that were numbered of the camp of Judah were a hundred and eighty-six thousand and four hundred, by their armies. They shall set forth first.* This particular verse in context is giving instructions as to how the Children of Israel were to organize themselves as they traveled through the desert on their way to the Promised Land. But once in the Promised Land, Judah did not always go first. God chose Gideon who was not only the least of his family but was from the least family in the tribe of Manasseh, not Judah, to lead Israel against the enemy (Judges 6:14).

"Send the worshippers out into battle first"

This instruction comes from the story of how Jehoshaphat was given victory over Moab and Ammon in 2 Chronicles 20. As believers, our entire life and everything we do should be an act of worship to the Lord. But as a spiritual warfare strategy, it doesn't always apply and could be disastrous if carried out in every battle. It worked for Jehoshaphat just that one time. We don't see this strategy used in any other battle described in scripture. If we apply this strategy for spiritual warfare every time, why don't we also use the strategy of attaching firebrands between two fox tails (Judges 15:4)? Ridiculous? Of course! And so is the assumption that any particular battle strategy should be followed every single time.

"The leader of the church/prayer group/ nation will receive the strategy for war"

This is not always true as the above story about Jehoshaphat's victory shows. It was the prophet Jahaziel who gave the strategy, not Jehoshaphat. In fact, it was the King who not only told the people, *Believe in the Lord your God, and you shall be established; believe His prophets and you shall prosper* (2 Chronicles 20:20). He then went on to consult with the people for consensus before giving the final orders for battle (vs. 21).

Two more examples

The Law said the showbread from the altar was not to be eaten by the common man. Yet the Priest gave it to David and his men when they were hungry (1 Samuel 21:3-6). The Law said don't work on the Sabbath, yet Jesus allowed His hungry disciples to go into the wheat fields and crack open some grains of wheat on the Sabbath, using the example of David and his men eating showbread (Matthew 12:1-5).

Are you getting the picture? It's not that worshipping first is wrong or that a pastor or ministry leader can't or shouldn't receive strategy. The point is that we need to realize that with God, there are no such set protocols. How we do what we do can and probably will differ, at least from time to time. It all depends on what God wants, not what worked in the past for us or anyone else. We shouldn't just pick and choose to do what we want when it comes to warfare strategy - or anything else. Many of God's instructions are foundational and set in concrete. Nevertheless, God is a God of variety. He's always creating. He likes to make stars, planets, people, snowflakes, kittens, and fingerprints. Yet none of them are identical. He is infinitely creative. So it is with patterns,

> *It all depends on what God wants, not what worked in the past.*

plans, and strategies for our prayer lives and for how we are to deal with our physical, emotional, and spiritual issues. It's the same for spiritual warfare strategies. Interestingly, when you study each of Jesus' recorded healing miracles, you will find that He never healed exactly the same way twice. Neither should we go into a spiritual battle with what worked yesterday. We need to get direction from God every time and be open to His variety of strategies and methods.

One Saturday night we had a special concert at our church at which a man and his wife sang beautifully. During one solo, in particular, the anointing of God fell on the man as he sang, making the number powerful and moving. It was awesome as the Presence of God filled the auditorium. The next morning the pastor asked him to sing it again, expecting the same result. It didn't happen. In fact, the song fell so flat it left the congregation disappointed because it ruined the delicious memory of the night before. We don't want that to happen to either our personal times of prayer or any prayer assignment we may engage in. So, watch out for the ruts in your life and in your spiritual warfare strategies. Always . . .

Wait for God's specific instructions:

- Listen
- Ask how
- Ask where
- Ask when

Every time!

18

PREEMPTIVE PRAYER AND PRAISE

Preemption is an action taken to go before another action. If you preempt something, you are putting something ahead of something else that was scheduled to take place. For example, if a person bought land before anyone else had a chance to make a bid on that land, we would say that he preempted the land purchase. Radio and television stations follow a pre-arranged schedule. But when something unexpected happens, news coverage of the tragedy preempts the schedule.

This word is used a lot in warfare. A preemptive action is a strike or attack carried out to prevent something else from happening. Especially something that will potentially cause harm. It may be used to prevent something that is both anticipated and feared. It is a preventative, a deterrent designed to gain the upper hand over an enemy.

To be proactive means to prepare for, intervene in, or control an expected occurrence or situation. To be preemptive is to take action against something possible, anticipated, and feared.

Job was preemptive when *he would rise early in the morning and offer burnt offerings according to the number of them all* (his children). For Job said, *It may be that my sons have sinned and cursed God in their hearts* (Job 1:5).

As he later admitted, he did this out of fear (Job 3:25), but it was, nevertheless, a preemptive action. He was doing something to prevent the possibility of something else from happening.

Putting on the armor of God is a preemptive action (Ephesians 6:14-17). It is both a preemptive and proactive thing to do. It is proactive because it is so that we *may be able to stand against the wiles of the devil* (vs. 11). It is preemptive when we actually stand against the devil before he attacks.

After putting the armor on, we are told to pray *always with all prayer and supplication in the Spirit, being watchful to this end with all perseverance and supplication* (Ephesians 6:18). The wording of this instruction lets us know that the prayers we pray after putting on the armor are not to be prayers about something that's already happened. They are watchful prayers looking for what's coming or what might come.

We are to be people of the possibility. We know how to do this when it comes to positive things, except that we usually call it dreaming.

> *We are to be people of the possibility.*

When we move past our dreams, putting faith, action, blood, sweat, and tears into the dream, we become a visionary. The world celebrates visionaries – as well they should.

We also consider the possibility of negative stuff. The problem is that when we consider the possible bad, painful, and negative, we often end up walking in fear and getting ourselves so worked up that we become paralyzed, frantic, depressed, totally useless, and make those around us miserable too. This is not pleasing to God and it causes our prayers to be nullified.

So, what do we do? Most people either deny the negative or they refuse to look at it, not wanting to see the possibility of evil. "Oh, just look on the bright side," we're told. And we should. But looking on the bright side should not exclude us from seeing the dark side at the same time. Paul told us to be watchful in our praying. Watchful for what? Watchful for what the principalities, powers, and rulers of the darkness are doing and planning to do. Watchful for what God is doing. It's not either/or. It's both/and.

Many believers today tend to rely on the prophetic word, dreams, and visions to tell us what is coming and what to expect. This is good and should be utilized more than ever. Because of a prophetic word about a storm coming in New Jersey, prayer teams took that word seriously and pray-walked up and down the New Jersey coastline, using every strategy God gave them. We don't even want to imagine how much worse Hurricane Sandy would have been without those preemptive prayers.

There was also a prophetic word about an explosion in Boston. Because of this word in 2011, Jon and Jolene Hamil of Lamplighter Ministries took steps to be preemptive in their ministry toward Boston. They sought God as to how to be proactive with this word. Following God's instructions, when the physical explosions occurred, they and their team were prepared for the explosion of the Spirit in Boston. Many churches were already connecting with each other. Immediately after the bombing, a website was up and running so that needs and resources could be easily connected – those who needed meals or a place to stay connected to the people willing to feed and/or house them, etc. All of that would not have happened if the people of God had not been preemptive in following up on the prophetic word.

However, the prophetic word should not be the only way to find out about the need for preemptive action. Our very prayers are to be preemptive. Everything available to us, including study, research, and deductive reasoning must also be used. Years ago, Doris Wagner developed a method for taking people through deliverance based on deductive reasoning. She did this because she saw the need to help people get free, felt the call of God to do something about it, yet didn't have the gift of discerning of spirits. After many success stories, primarily with pastors and Christian leaders, she began to teach others a method of deliverance by deductive reasoning that God gave her. I took her training; it is very involved and takes a lot longer than it would if the spiritual gift of discerning of spirits was used. But it is still very effective. It works.

The same is true concerning preemptive prayer. Yes, we're to seek the gift of prophecy and we need a seer anointing. But according to Ephesians 6:18, we're also to be watchful. Watchful of what? Of what's going on in the world. Of what the possibilities are. We need to exercise perseverance in watching.

Jesus said, *If you will not watch, I will come upon you as a thief, and you will not know what hour I will come upon you* (Revelation 3:3).

The result of being watchful is that it will make us either fearful or faithful. In Judges 7, God gave Gideon a prophetic word about coming against the Midianites. He said, *But if you are afraid to go down, go down to the camp with Purah your servant and you shall hear what they say; and afterward your hands shall be strengthened to go down against the camp* (Judges 7:10-11).

Being fearful to act on the prophetic word, Gideon took God's advice. He took Purah, snuck down to the Midianite camp and listened. He did something and extended some effort to receive the confirmation God encouraged him to get and to know what was going on. After God's instruction was confirmed, Gideon devised a clever preemptive plan and told his men to watch and do what he did. The result was a resounding victory. Lesson: We need to watch what is going on in the world as well as what God is doing in it.

That was preemption in physical warfare. In 2 Kings 11, there is an interesting story of a preemptive act in spiritual warfare. After King Ahaziah, king of Judah was killed, his mother Athaliah destroyed all the royal heirs and took the throne for herself. What she didn't know was that Ahaziah's sister took her own preemptive action by hiding her brother's one-year-old son, Johash. First, he was hidden in a bedroom, then in the house of the Lord for six years. When the boy was seven years old, Jehoiada the priest took preemptive action to make him king and get rid of Athaliah. He brought him out with armed escorts who literally surrounded the child on all sides so that he could be crowned king in place of his grandmother. After the crowning, of course, Athaliah found out about it, threw a fit, and was killed. The result of this secret, preemptive strategy was that a covenant was made between the Lord, the newly-crowned king, and the people. The altars to Baal were broken in pieces, the city was quiet, and Johash did what was right in the sight of the Lord all the days in which his mentor, Jehoiada the priest, instructed him.

This is an excellent example of preemptive prayer that resulted in preemptive action. Tragedy happened. But preemptive action took place, followed by six years of preemptive prayer. It was prayer focused on a final outcome, rather than based on the current state of affairs. The result was victory, not only for the rightful heir to the throne, but for the people of the land and the will of the Lord.

These two stories about Gideon and Johash show that we need to pray preemptively for each other and our world. We need to pray preemptively into prophecy. We also need to arm ourselves and surround each other as children of the King, so that each member of the Body of Christ can take their rightful place in the kingdom, doing whatever job it is that God has assigned and equipped them to do.

2 Chronicles 23:6 says in part, *All the people shall keep the watch of the Lord.* Keeping the watch of the Lord isn't just about looking to see what

is going on right now; it is about looking to see what is coming – what has been prophesied for the future.

When the walls around Jerusalem were being rebuilt, the Arabs, the Ammonites, and the Ashdodites conspired together to, not only attack Jerusalem, but also create confusion (Nehemiah 4:7-8; 7:3). Therefore, Nehemiah set a watch both day and night. Some of these watchmen gave praise and thanks to the Lord *watch by watch* (Nehemiah 12:24).

Thus, we see preemptive praise and thanksgiving. Preemptive praise and thanksgiving give God the glory for His answers to our prayers as if they've already been answered and thanking Him as if it's already done. Preemptive thanksgiving is taking our petitions and converting them into expressions of praise. Doing this lays a foundation for present tense blessing. It also counteracts apathy. How can you be apathetic when you're worshipping God and thanking Him for your future as well as your present situation? Preemptive praise and thanksgiving keep you on an even keel spiritually so that you don't become distraught when bad things happen. When we get into the habit of preemptive prayer and thanksgiving, we are able to immediately get into prayer for all the good that God is going to bring out of such tragedies for the sake of the Kingdom of Heaven! It enables us to see that while evil does exist and bad things happen, God is able to rule and overrule. We can see this truth over and over in the pages of scripture. We can see it in our modern-day events.

Look at how the Holocaust prepared the Jews to cry out for their own land. Years before, in the late 1800s, prophecy-believing Christians had discerned the times and knew that it was time for Jews to return to the Promised Land. But most Jews were comfortably entrenched in the various countries their families had been dispersed into years and years before. Notwithstanding, the Christian's preemptive prayers led them to preemptive action. They began to establish a witness for Yeshua in Israel and to help the Jews to not only move, but to live a better life once there. Unfortunately, the majority of Jews had to be motivated by fear to be willing to move. Was the need to escape from danger really how God wanted them to go back to the Promised Land? Of course not. But God looks long-range. He'll allow our sins and lack of preemptive thinking to back us into a corner for His own purposes, the betterment of the Kingdom, and for our good.

19

PRAYING FOR GOVERNMENT

Blessed be the Lord my Rock, who trains my hands for war and my fingers for battle (Psalm 144:1).

He teaches my hands to make war, so that my arms can bend a bow of bronze (Psalm 18:34).

He teaches my hands for the war, so that my arms can bend a bow of bronze (2 Samuel 22:35).

The need to pray for our government, national, state, and local, is something on which everyone seems to agree. Especially since we are specifically told to do so (1 Timothy 2:2). But how, exactly, should we do this? As I've walked the path of being a governmental intercessor for more than 25 years, I've learned the importance of the three scriptures at the beginning of this chapter. They tell me that if my hands are going to be trained for the spiritual warfare involved in praying for government, I absolutely must be teachable and willing to change how I do things. In the process, this chapter is all about the guidelines the Lord has shown me that are essential for effectively praying for government - or anything else for that matter.

PROTOCOL – First, we need to recognize that the protocol for corporate prayer needs to be different than the freedom we have in our personal prayer times. The focus of the group needs to be determined and every participant needs to agree to stay within the boundaries of the chosen focus. If a group is formed to pray for personal needs, that's great. But if its focus is to be government, then it's not the place to pray for Aunt Sally or Uncle Joe, or even your church. Those needs can be prayed for before or after the pre-determined group prayer time, but not during the time specifically designated for government.

Once the focus has been set, the guidelines found in Chapter 16, Disciplined Intercession for Groups, need to be followed.

The protocol for each particular assignment is usually different and needs to be specified. For example, when permission is given to pray in a particular room of a government building, the rules given by the governmental authority must be followed. An "undercover assignment" in a building, a city location, or another country is something else. My husband and I engage in a lot of undercover assignments. When others are with us, we require strict adherence to the rules pertaining to how to remain in stealth mode. Unfortunately, there are prayer ministries that send people out to pray on-site without such guidelines. We participated in one such assignment that proved to be disastrous. As directed by the leader, we entered a bus that was to drive us around to various embassies in Washington, DC. We were supposed to get off the bus and pray around the buildings on the public sidewalks while acting like tourists. Regardless, having received no guidelines, one man took his perceived authority too far. In his boldness and immaturity, he literally shouted decrees and declarations at various embassies. The result was that our presence was perceived as a threat and the police were called. Our assignment came to an abrupt, premature end because the guidelines weren't clearly communicated to the entire team.

When a prayer meeting is over, there needs to be sealing prayer so that whatever was of God is protected against demonic theft. In addition, there needs to be prayer against retaliation and retribution toward all those involved in the prayer group or assignment. I like to specifically include their families, homes, vehicles, resources, and everything that concerns them.

ACCOUNTABILITY - This is key as you can tell if you've read the previous chapters. It is crucial not only because you need backup prayer but because you need their input. A transparent, teachable intercessor should never be afraid of accountability.

Participants in prayer for government must be willing to learn the rules of spiritual warfare if they want to be accountable to, or in agreement with, scripture. I've seen too many people quote 1 John 4:4 about *greater is He who is in me* and go after principalities and powers by themselves and get attacked by the enemy as a result. First of all, they ignore the fact that the context of this verse is all about warfare guidelines. We need to always remain teachable and search out other passages for guidance.

For example, too many people teach that we should put on the pieces of armor listed in Ephesians 6: 13 every morning. I am strongly opposed to that teaching because I have yet to find biblical instruction that we are ever to take it off! As intercessors, we need to just "straighten it" before we go to bed and again when we arise the next morning. Our satanic enemy knows how vulnerable Christians make themselves when they go to sleep thinking that their job of intercession is done for the day. We are called to be warriors, not fighters. As a Vietnam veteran told me years ago, "A fighter fights in a battle, then goes home. A warrior is always on duty."

FORGIVENESS - Forgiveness of those who have allowed themselves to be tools of Satan is key to governmental prayer. We cannot afford to harbor anger, bitterness, or resentment. No matter what scripture they claim, I have yet to meet anyone who held "righteous indignation" as Jesus did when He tossed out the money-changers from the temple. Yes, He acted in anger, but a few days later, He gave His life for those very people. A person with true "righteous indignation" is willing to literally give their life in exchange for those they are angry with. Forgiveness does not include compromise. In any political environment, forgiveness with no compromise can be very difficult. But, with God's help, we can do whatever He asks us to do. It is our choice as to whether we obey or not. It helps to remember that forgiveness is more about us and our attitude than it is about the other person. When we forgive, we take our hands off and let God deal with them.

> *Forgiveness is key to governmental prayer.*

Often our anger results from not knowing the facts or language difficulties. According to quantum physics, all matter retains memory. This fact affects our ability to hear God. How does that affect those in government? Here's an example. A good person is newly elected to office in our city, state, or national government. They are often given an office that was formerly occupied by an ungodly office-holder. The office needs to be cleansed with prayer prior to the newly elected official taking occupancy. When I teach on this subject, I sometimes use the example of when a relatively good man was put into a national position. At first, when he had major decisions to make, he would retreat to his personal home for contemplation. Consequently, he made good decisions. But one day he invited a leader from a country that has purposefully and legally legislated God out of their national life, to come stay in his house. The foreign leader stayed several days. When the foreign leader left, the home was not cleansed of all the ungodly spiritual contamination the visitor left behind. From that point on the leader began making unwise decisions that were not in the best interest of our nation. Probably every national governmental leader has operated in the same ignorance of how quantum physics affects their environment and ability to make good decisions. Our job as governmental intercessors is to cover them when they are ignorant. We need to be aware of what's happening with our leaders whether we're called to pray for our local government, our state government, or our national government.

Forgiveness needs to be balanced by God's specific direction as well as scriptural directives. We need to forgive people for their actions or words against us personally, but we need to separate that from the unrighteous actions of leaders who make decisions on behalf of a group of people. Let me explain. While many iniquitous government workers operate out of ignorance, in the age in which we are now living, many government workers of iniquity know exactly what they are doing. They have been presented with a choice as to whether to serve God or Satan and have chosen Satan and his ways. I don't believe we can know for certain who these people are unless they literally, physically, and publicly bow before a false god. However, I believe strongly that we need to be very careful before using Christ's words on the cross to *forgive them for they know not what they do* (Luke 23:34). Why would I say such a thing? I touched on this in Chapter 17, Warfare Ruts.

Nevertheless, look at scripture:

- God is the One who caused Egypt to hate the Jews (Psalm 105:25).
- We are told that God will choose the delusions of the wicked (Isaiah 66:4, 2 Thessalonians 2:9-12).
- At one point God said, *Do not pray for this people nor lift up a cry or prayer for them, nor make intercession to Me; for I will not hear you* (Jeremiah 7:16, Jeremiah 11:14).
- Jesus pronounced *woe* on various cities then let us know that we are judged by the level of enlightenment we have, not the level of evil (Matthew 11:21-24).

Every prayer is predicated on hearing God!

We can't know the heart of another or what level of enlightenment they've had. Furthermore, we don't know what God is doing or how He is using them. The Egyptian Pharaoh is a good example. He had a choice. Unfortunately, for him and his nation, he made the wrong choice. But God used that choice for His own purposes. So, when we automatically pray to forgive a governmental leader because of their ignorance, we could be interfering in God's dealings with them. Jesus knew the specific people who crucified Him. He knew they were ignorant. We don't always know this. With our hearts full of personal forgiveness, we can pray for God to intervene in their lives but a blanket prayer is not appropriate. Only He knows the end from the beginning. As in all situations, we must always ask God how we are to pray.

WORDS - Our words are absolutely critical when it comes to praying for, and talking about, government. I have repented many times for words I used to say in a joking manner pertaining to the federal government. When God began to pull me into specializing in national government, I had to change my ways and become open for Him to teach me and reveal truth to me. Now I try to watch my words. Have you ever noticed that when people run out of good arguments or facts to back up their views, they get into name-calling? When believers resort to name-calling, we descend to Satan's level. You probably know as many or more scriptures than I do about how Christians are to build up and plant rather than tear down and destroy. Name-calling is a form of cursing. We are told to bless, not curse (Romans 12:14).

RESEARCH - Everyone needs godly, scripture-based discernment and knowledge. This often requires research. Most don't like to do the research because we're comfortable with our own mindset or that of our favorite news outlet, talk-show host, friends, or social media.

Sometimes we need to learn about the culture peculiar to a specific location. For example, the culture of New York City is different than the culture of East Texas. We can't pray out of a heart of love (which is God's language) if we show contempt for a particular culture or refuse to appreciate where they're coming from. For example, people who grow up and continue to live in a city don't understand rural areas. Many of them don't have an appreciation for the land. When we lived in Dallas, we had friends who grumbled when it rained on weekends. They had no appreciation for how badly the farmers needed the rain in order to produce the meat and vegetables that graced the tables of those who grumbled.

In 2004 Gary and I took a small group of people on an undercover prayer assignment to Israel. Meeting beforehand to prepare them for cultural differences, one woman was shocked when we told her that she would not find a convenience store on every corner from which to purchase bottled water day or night.

On one of our trips to India to visit the boy's home we helped establish, we were invited to eat at the home of the administrator. We both ate all of the food that we were served. The next thing I knew, our host was heaping another helping of rice on our plates. I'd been taught as a child that good manners meant that you ate all the food on your plate no matter who put it there. Plus, I didn't want to insult his wife's cooking. Though already full, I forced myself to eat the second helping of rice as well. Much to my surprise, he gave me a third helping and . . . well, honestly, I don't remember how many servings of rice I received. Finally, I was so full, I felt sick. I couldn't eat rice again for a very long time. Only much later, did I learn that, at least in that part of India, good manners required you to leave a small amount of uneaten food on your plate as an indication that you were finished.

In some countries, it is assumed that if you go to a store that is full of people, most don't recognize or employ the idea of a line. In America, pushing and shoving others can get you thrown out of the store or even arrested if you are too aggressive. Here, the protocol is to stand in line and wait your turn.

We were blessed to host a state and national leader of the Hispanic community in our home. He was an immigrant who had obtained US citizenship. Based on his experience, his cry was for all immigrants to learn the basis of our American culture. Assuming the American culture is the same as their country of origin, immigrants often do things in ignorance that can alienate them from others or even get them in trouble with the law. This is true about immigrants in any country. Ask questions. If you don't know what to ask, do some research.

I've used examples from other countries for a reason. If an intercessor is not employed in government themselves, they need to approach it as if it is a foreign place. That is because the culture of government differs from typical American life. During my senior year of college, I had a teacher who was remarkably effective. One of my classmates asked him why he was so much better than his colleagues. "When you graduate from school and begin to teach, you gradually lose the perspective of the student," he said. "So, as a student, make a list of what you believe makes for a good and effective teacher. Then refer back to that list through the years of your career because you will eventually forget what it feels like to be a student." That is wise advice for any career but is essential for governmental employees. Unfortunately, many in government lose the perspective of the common man. An astute intercessor must take this into consideration when praying for government.

TONGUES - The gift of tongues is a valuable tool to use when praying for government. I Corinthians 14:1 instructs us to seek the spiritual gifts. This is one of them. Get it. Use it. I recently read an appeal by a national leader for individuals and prayer groups to spend up to an hour praying in tongues whenever we gather together because the current issues are so complex. This, I believe, is worth considering.

PRAYING FOR GOVERNMENT

OVERVIEW - When praying for government, get an overview of where you're going in prayer. To do this, we must look at and deal with reality. Two examples are Presidents Bush and Obama. Both received a lot of prayer during their presidency. But much of the prayer didn't take into consideration important aspects in their backgrounds, training, and involvement in activities counter to what they needed for such a position. Instead, the majority of prayers had to do with what they said, did, or where they went.

BOUNDARIES - Know what your boundaries are and don't go beyond them. We had a teacher I'll call Sue, who went with a group on a prayer journey to Washington, DC. Their assignment was to pray over various governmental departments. The last night of the assignment the leader realized that they had not prayed over a particular building. Sue simply wanted to return to her hotel room and go to bed. But her partner felt led to volunteer to go pray over that last building. When the two women arrived outside the building, they began to pray. Unfortunately, instead of staying on the public sidewalk, Sue stepped onto the grounds of the building without the call to do so as her partner had. Sue returned home from the assignment and was sick for a week. Her partner was the one who received the call from the Lord to pray at that location. Sue's job was to support her, not to do the same things.

I once had to tell a friend with serious illnesses to stop praying about all the national and world news she heard on the television. Not only was she ill-equipped spiritually to handle every governmental problem she heard about, but she also was not physically strong enough to do so. God had given her a particular focus for her prayers, and she needed to stay within the boundaries of that focus.

National and world governmental issues are usually tied in with principalities and powers. Dealing with such is a group effort and only with a specific leading and strategy from the Lord. Not something you come against by yourself. For example, many intercessors want to come against a spirit that is a world principality. Doing so is as foolhardy as it would have been to send one man to take down the entire Nazi regime during World War 2. Such a person would have been set up for certain failure. So it is with ruling spirits. I've talked to enough people who suffered great loss physically, mentally, financially, and relationally as a result of trying to take on a territorial or world spirit by themselves. I've heard stories of some who have even lost their lives. That's why it's critical that we know our boundaries and stay within them.

EGO - When I first got into the city-wide prayer effort, I discovered a lot of ego on the part of prayer ministry leaders and members. When the various ministries got together, I heard people bragging about how they'd participated with big-name spiritual leaders of the day. How many prayer journeys they'd been on. How their assignments were more important than others. When it comes to prayer - or any ministry for that matter - there is no place for ego. We need to know our place, stay there, and be satisfied until or unless God promotes us. Consider David's top mighty men. There were the top three, the next three, and the thirty. Abishai was the head of the second three. He was "*most honored*" but didn't attain the position of one of the top three. Benaiah was "*more honored*" than the thirty, but wasn't one of the first three. Yet they were all valuable and mighty men of valor. All positions within David's army were needed. All were important. Status is of no spiritual importance in the long run. What is important is letting go of our ego and our pride, so we can do whatever it is that God wants us to do.

Besides, being a hidden intercessor is a good place to be because you come under less attack. So, keep on praying. Learn the rules of warfare. And keep learning. You are needed, wanted, and valuable!

20

PRAYER JOURNEY GUIDELINES

Though the term "prayer journey" has been used in various chapters of this book, an explanation is that it is simply taking a trip of any length so that you are able to stand in the locality of the target of your prayers. Some refer to it as "praying on-site with insight." It can be a short distance across town or a trip of several days across the nation or around the world. Truly, things look different when you are actually looking at what you are praying for or about. Especially if you've done research about the place in advance. When I took a team of intercessors to pray at a historical site in Dallas, Texas and told them about its history, one woman later said, "I will never look at 'The Old Red Courthouse' the same way."

Here is a list of "do's and don'ts" that I've learned through the years that will make your prayer journeys more enjoyable and fruitful.

Prepare in advance, both physically and spiritually, for the assignment. Do historical research on the places you are going to visit. Determine what you are supposed to take with you. You may be prompted by the Holy Spirit to take things that are needed for worship or prophetic acts – a tambourine, salt, bread, wine, trumpet, banners. Give a copy of your research to the leader in advance. If they want, be prepared to give a copy to all other participants also.

Take your Bible, paper, and pen with you. But, if the journey is an undercover assignment, do not take your Bible out in public. If need be, download a Bible app on your phone and use that.

Arrive at the meeting place early, ready to go.

Don't wait for the leader to say, "Let's go" to decide you need to go to the bathroom. Take care of your personal needs in such a way as to not inconvenience the entire group. Emergencies call for exceptions but don't cause one by being inconsiderate of others or not thinking ahead.

Double-check all forms of transportation - airline departures, rental cars, etc. If driving, make sure vehicles are adequately prepared for the journey. A woman on a team I led one time volunteered to drive her SUV. Unfortunately, she did not have enough gasoline for the journey and had to stop to fill up. Consequently, everyone who rode with her missed a critical part of the assignment.

Pray with your eyes open unless your group is not around other people. "Religious" behavior is inappropriate and unnecessary. Our son made a mission trip to a country where praying openly is illegal. Wanting to pray before meals, they simply raised their glasses as if they were making a toast and smiled at each other while one team member said a prayer of thanks.

Quietly check any guidance you receive with the leader before speaking it out to the entire group. If you want to include a specific site, talk to the leader first and let them announce it to the group. If possible, tell the leader before the journey. If they say no, don't complain about it to others or go behind their back.

Acknowledge that the leader knows more about the assignment than you do. They are also responsible for the group's schedule, the safety and well-being of others, and directions given by those in authority over them. Extend him or her grace. In other words, don't try to take control of the journey, or act like a know-it-all. At the last minute, I was asked to take over the leadership of a conference in India. One member of the team did everything she could to sabotage my leadership. She did not know that the local leaders had given me guidelines as to what we were to do and not do. I relayed those guidelines to the team, but she refused to follow them. She even manipulated other team members to secretly do what the local leader had forbidden. The result was division, discord, and confusion. The team left India feeling disheartened.

Be sensitive to those who are less experienced in taking prayer journeys, as well as, those who are more experienced. Kindness and grace go a long way.

Do not talk about past assignments so as to cause those who did not experience them to feel inferior or excluded. There is no place for hierarchy among intercessors. Make a point of including people who are new to you. Prayer journeys are no place for cliques or egos.

Stay focused, even when traveling together to another location. Listen to praise music, talk about the assignment, pray in tongues, whatever it takes to stay focused. And remember, mealtimes are not a break. You are on serious business for the King. Act like the ambassador you are. An assignment I led required the team to travel in multiple vehicles. I found out later that a person in another car monopolized the entire trip to our destination with the value of buying gold as an investment. The result was that the people in his vehicle were scattered in their prayers and had trouble focusing on the objective of the assignment.

Be careful of people you meet along the way. Are you to talk to them? What do you share, if anything? Are you to minister to them or they to you? What is God saying through them? We stopped for lunch on a day-long prayer journey. At the restaurant, we met some people who said they were Christians. Before I knew it, my enthusiastic team was telling them all about what we were doing, why, and where we were going. I was aghast. No one had any idea if the strangers really were Christians or if they understood or agreed with such a prayer journey. The group made all of us vulnerable to attack, curses, and soulish prayers.

Avoid religious grammar with those you meet. When you find out they are believers or members of a church, don't assume they understand what you're doing and why. Let them talk.

Do not go on a prayer journey without a flexible schedule. Leaders try to estimate how long it will take but they don't know what God will do, or if there will be an unavoidable delay of some kind. People on prayer journeys must be flexible and prepared for anything. One man decided to travel to a local site with team members instead of taking his own car. His schedule was not flexible; he had to be at work by a certain time. Consequently, everyone in that vehicle had to miss part of the prayer assignment. If it is a journey of several nights, always pack enough vitamins, medicine, underwear, and so forth, for extra days. I was delayed on one trip for 24 hours because striking airline workers were burning tires on the runways the day I was supposed to depart. Another time, our luggage didn't arrive until the day after we landed. And I don't even remember how many times we have had to sit in an airport terminal all night due to something out of our control. Any kind of travel needs to be viewed as an adventure where anything can happen. So, go with joy and a great deal of flexibility. A Jewish friend said that a "new" beatitude was recently discovered. "Blessed are the flexible, for they shall not be bent out of shape."

You shouldn't join the group late or leave the group early without advance permission from the leader. Don't assume that doing so will be alright. Latecomers often interrupt the focus of the group and the flow of the Spirit.

If the leader has designated a co-leader, be aware that the two leaders probably have divided responsibilities. Pay attention to who has responsibility for what. They also may not have had a chance to communicate all information with each other. Direct questions about what you are doing, why, and if you can do something additional, to the primary leader only. Do not play the two against each other or try to manipulate the co-leader to let you do something that the leader has already said no to. I began leading prayer journeys while Gary was still working full time and only able to join me once in a while. When he did, because he was a man, and my husband, team members "assumed" that he was the co-leader. In truth, he was still learning about prayer journeys and sometimes gave wrong answers and permissions. Such behavior put me in the awkward position of maintaining the integrity and focus of the assignment while trying to honor my husband.

Your leader will make mistakes. Extend grace.

Others will be insensitive and do things wrong. Extend grace to them. A prayer journey is not the time or place to get offended, become frustrated or angry, or to gripe about each other. Instead, it is a time to be flexible, kind, and focused on the Lord - not others in the group.

Unless you are truly sick, don't tell the leader you "feel" that the Lord does not want you to participate in a portion of the journey. God sent you on the assignment to work with the group, not to be a lone ranger or to draw attention to yourself.

Drink plenty of water. Staying hydrated is imperative.

If you have a medical condition that requires a set time for food intake, carry snacks with you. Don't insist that the whole group cater to your needs. And don't assume that you always will be able to stop at a store to buy what you need.

If the journey is one of several days and you have a medical condition (high blood pressure, diabetes, hypoglycemia, epilepsy, etc.) make sure the leader(s) and your roommate know about it. After an entire ministry team had boarded an airplane to Russia, the wife of Gary's roommate told me that her husband took medication for epilepsy. Neither she, nor I, were going on the trip. We were simply at the airport to see them off. "Does the leader know this?" I asked. The answer was, "No." I immediately asked the ticket agent to pull Gary off the plane for just a moment so I could tell him. Someone on that team needed to know about that man's health issue in case of an unforeseen event.

If you are exhausted, rest. Take advantage of opportunities to sit down. Let your leader know of any physical limitations you have during the planning stages of the journey. A good leader will help you evaluate whether or not you should join the team on that particular assignment.

Keep your leader informed about individual conversations with locals and any incident that happens to you. It may reveal critical pieces to the puzzle of what God is doing.

Keep God's secrets. Only share with others what God allows you to share, and no more.

Other Vawtermark Publications

Focus! Fight! Finish! and *The Giving Book* are available only from the author. For more information on cost and how to order, send an email to **info@vawtermark.com.**

FOCUS! FIGHT! FINISH!
Prerequisites to Spiritual Warfare
RaJean Thayer Vawter

Spiritual victory requires focus. But how do you become focused? How do you fight the good fight of faith without going around in circles? Can you ensure that you will fulfill your purpose and destiny God has for you? In *Focus! Fight! Finish!*, RaJean Thayer Vawter gives practical answers to these questions that are applicable in any culture, anytime, anywhere. This little volume will challenge, encourage and help you gain the victory you desire. It can change your life!

There are many books and teaching manuals on the subjects like; prayer and intercession, spiritual warfare, etc. ***Focus! Fight! Finish!*** *is unique and covers many points on practical application. I found it so important that I have introduced her to teaching our leaders and members of the 12,000 plus churches in India, and we are translating the book into many Indian languages. Her teaching online is recorded and has become part of our online course.*

Abraham Sekhar
Leader of Spirit-filled Churches of India
And Global Apostolic Transformation Missions

THE GIVING BOOK
What Your Pastor Won't Tell You
RaJean Thayer Vawter

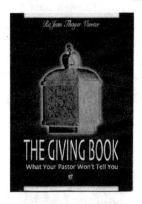

In *The Giving Book*, RaJean Thayer Vawter takes on a sensitive topic with fresh, thought-provoking enthusiasm. She points out the inconsistencies of some of the most prevalent 'doctrines' on tithing and other aspects of Christian giving. She faithfully supports all of her analysis with biblical references that breathe fresh life into perhaps one of the church's oldest and often most abused and misunderstood 'sacraments.' Readers will find very practical ways to leverage their giving into a more exciting and rewarding spiritual experience. She shows that our giving need not be born out of legalistic obligation but from a position of delight, freedom, and pure worship. She uncovers principles of giving from both the Old and New Testaments that the church has overlooked for too long.

The Giving Book is revolutionizing our thinking in the sensitive and important subject of giving tithes to God (or to the church). But the facts mentioned cannot be ignored and I am personally blessed to know these facts. I recommend every leader reads this book.

Abraham Sekhar
Leader of Spirit-filled Churches of India
And Global Apostolic Transformation Missions

Rose is available on Amazon.com and other online bookstores in paperback, hardback, and Kindle editions.

ROSE
A Young Girl's Grit and Grace During World War II
Gary E. Vawter

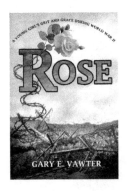

Little Rose Brezina had a cheerful spirit that brought joy into every experience. That spirit would soon be tested, though, as the Nazi army moved in and war came to her city. Before she would even reach her teens, Rose would lose her best friend, join an underground effort to hide Jews, and suffer repeated torture by a Gestapo determined to break her. And yet even though her home was destroyed, her baby brother killed, and her mother kidnapped, Rose knew God was with her and saw evidence of His faithfulness in the small things. In the end, World War II proved to be no match for this courageous little girl from Vienna, Austria.

Rose's story is so inspiring and Vawter does a wonderful job bringing it to life for the reader. I was brought to tears several times and I was touched by the way Rose relied on her faith in God to get through horrendous circumstances. Vawter's use of language is beautiful and impressive. In my opinion, **Rose** *should be required reading in schools.*

The Bookish Blonde
Bookstore Owner

CPSIA information can be obtained
at www.ICGtesting.com
Printed in the USA
LVHW021751250423
745294LV00029B/474